Sources of Stress and Relief for African American Women

Sources of Stress and Relief for African American Women

CATHERINE FISHER COLLINS

Race and Ethnicity in Psychology
Jean Lau Chin, John D. Robinson, and Victor De La Cancela,
Series Editors

Westport, Connecticut
London

Library of Congress Cataloging-in-Publication Data

Collins, Catherine Fisher.
   Sources of stress and relief for African American women / Catherine Fisher Collins.
     p. cm.—(Race and ethnicity in psychology, ISSN 1543–2203)
   Includes bibliographical references and index.
   ISBN 0–86569–267–X (alk. paper)
    1. Stress (Psychology) 2. Stress management for women. 3. African American
   women—Psychology. I. Title. II. Series.
   BF575.S75C57   2003
   155.9'042'082—dc21   2002193135

British Library Cataloguing in Publication Data is available.

Library of Congress Catalog Card Number: 2002193135
ISBN: 0–86569–267–X
ISSN: 1543–2203

First published in 2003

Praeger Publishers, 88 Post Road West, Westport, CT 06881
An imprint of Greenwood Publishing Group, Inc.
www.praeger.com

Printed in the United States of America

The paper used in this book complies with the
Permanent Paper Standard issued by the National
Information Standards Organization (Z39.48–1984).

10 9 8 7 6 5 4 3 2 1

Copyright Acknowledgments

The author and publisher gratefully acknowledge permission to use the following material:

Poem "To Dance" from Valada S. Flewellyn, *Poetically Just Us*, Parker Initiatives Publications, 1990.

Every reasonable effort has been made to trace the owners of copyright materials in this
book, but in some instances this has proven impossible. The author and publisher will be
glad to receive information leading to more complete acknowledgments in subsequent
printings of this book, and in the meantime extend their apologies for any omission.

Dedication
This book is dedicated to Janice M. Scott, a member of Jack and Jill of
America, Inc., Burke-Fairfax (VA) Chapter, who was among those who
perished at the Pentagon, Washington, D.C., on September 11, 2001

This book is also dedicated to all the victims of the attack on America on
September 11, 2001

Contents

Illustrations

Series Foreword

It is expected that nearly half of the entire U.S. population will be composed of ethnic and racial minorities by the year 2050. With this growing diversity, clinicians, researchers and, indeed, all Americans need to understand that the Eurocentric views particular to Caucasians may or may not be relevant or adequate to address mental health issues in racial and ethnic minorities. This series addresses those issues, aiming to better understand how these factors affect mental health, and what needs to be done, or done differently, to heal disorders that may arise.

Series Editors

Jean Lau Chin
Assistant Professor of Psychiatry
Center for Minority Training Program
Boston University School of Medicine
President Elect, Division of Women
American Psychological Association
President, CEO Services

Victor De La Cancela
Associate Clinical Professor
Medical Psychology
College of Physicians and Surgeons
Columbia University
Psychosocial faculty,
Beth Israel Medical Center
Clinical Psychologist, United States
    Army Reserve

John D. Robinson
Chief, Interdepartmental Training Programs
Departments of Psychiatry and Surgery
College of Medicine and Hospital
Howard University
Clinical Professor of Psychiatry,
Georgetown University School of Medicine

Preface

Each day African American women attempt to meet the challenges of their family, work, and community. All too often, in meeting these challenges, we engage in some form of behavior or action that may, in turn, generate some form of stress. Sometimes when we are feeling the effects of stress, we call it "getting on our last nerve" or "getting on our last reserved nerve." Whatever you choose to call it, stress can be harmful to your well-being and stress can do serious physical and psychological harm. In fact, as bell hooks states in her book *Sisters of the Yam* (1993, p. 53), "stress is a hidden killer underlying all major health problems black women face."

How long we live depends in part on how well we manage our stress—and we are losing the daily battles with stress, as evidenced by African American women's poor health status and their "1998 death rate of 589.4 per 100,000 as compared to White women's of 372.5 per 100,000" (Misra 2001, p. 65). The physiological and psychological reactions to stress impact our lives in many ways. This is not your typical book about stress; instead, it confronts from an Afrocentric perspective some of the real-life issues that are stressors for African American women. As presented in part I, some of the real-life stressors we encounter emanate from family, community, work, colleagues, and friends.

In part II, you will find ways to deal with these stressors. As we meet the new challenges of the twenty-first century, we bring with us all our experiences—some good and some bad. At the same time, African American women must build on the good experiences and moderate the effects of the bad experiences so that their physical and mental health status will improve.

There has been an attempt to suppress and monitor what African American women writers present in the printed media. Some African American women write about customs, heritage, and relationships from a cultural perspective, yet there are those who critique our work and make statements about what they think we should have said or written about ourselves. The information contained in these chapters is derived from an Afrocentric point of view and is meant to educate all.

I begin chapter 1 with a request for the reader to complete a short written stress test. This stress test will identify the reader's stress level. In chapter 2, the reader learns how stress affects the various physiological systems in the human body, how stress causes illnesses, and how stress impacts longevity. Current research that deals with African American women's health status will help to validate and verify the impact of stress. Chapter 3 focuses on family relationships and stressors at home, addressing how to manage the multiple stressors in family life and offering some valuable survival techniques.

Chapter 4 spotlights stressors related to the work environment. Specifically, utilizing a historical framework, chapter 4 examines stress created by the relationships between black women and white and black males and females in the workplace and community. White Americans hold some of this nation's top-level positions in the workforce. For example, 98.3 percent of airplane pilots are white; 95.6 percent of dentists are white; 86.5 percent of college faculty members are white; 93.9 percent of published authors are white; 93.8 percent of lawyers are white; and 91.9 percent of economists are white (Woods 1998). With so many of the top positions held by white Americans, the "concrete ceiling" is reached pretty early in the career path of African American females. Several case studies are included to illustrate the decaying working relationships between black and white women in the workplace. Racism, sexism, and cultural differences are also addressed as sources of stress.

In addition, chapter 4 presents the findings of a survey commissioned by *Essence* magazine on how African American women are dealing with many stressful situations. Each of the following three chapters reports on various studies to illustrate how participants are dealing with stress-induced situations in the hope that readers will gain some insight into problem-solving techniques.

Chapter 5 describes the stress African American women may experience as members of various female-led organizations. As members of these organizations, African American women may create stress; as leaders of these organizations, they must respond to stresses brought on by members.

In part II I begin with the suggestion that all African American women determine whether they are heart healthy and describe my own experience with a cardio-lite stress test. In chapter 6 I describe the stress-busting benefits of movement, from bicycling to roller-skating and skipping, just to mention a few. Chapter 7 shows the mind-body connection and the benefits of biofeedback, visualization, and the de-grudging exercises and how the power of prayer can help African American women manage stressful life events. Chapter 8 explores how spas, messages, and watsu can act as stress busters as well as delving into the benefits of aromatherapy, herbs, and juices. It also includes a Stress Busters chart. Chapter 9 examines the strong social support system at home and how work in the community can be both stressful and beneficial. The book concludes with a Stress Reduction Contract for Life (SRCL). The SRCL includes a section for readers to list their stressors and how they intend to deal with them.

I sincerely hope that readers will enjoy this book, will begin to identify and control unmanageable stressors by using some of the fortifying behaviors presented here, and will live more productive and far less stressful lives.

Acknowledgments

I wish first to thank God for the many blessings that made this book possible.

To my wonderful son, Clyde, and my daughter, Laura Harris, her husband, Kenneth, and grandchildren Kenneth and Crystal—thank you. Each of you are so special in my life. Sister, Fay, and Brother, David—hugs and kisses.

For the technical support from Glendora Johnson-Cooper, librarian, and Elizabeth Webber—a very special thank you. To my colleagues at the State University of New York, Empire State College, and the State University of New York at Buffalo Women Studies Department, I also extend thanks. My sisters, in the Buffalo Chapter of Links, Eastern Star Naomi Chapter#10 PHA, For Women Only, Hadji Court 62#, Daughters of Isis, and members of Jack and Jill of America Inc., Buffalo Chapter and Foundation—thank you for letting me be a part of these outstanding organizations. To everyone I forgot, know that you are all very special to me and to my life.

PART I

The Effects of Stress on Your Life

The status of African American women's health has been historically poor over the past fifty years. Even minimal health improvements have not been made at any significant level. Some believe that the lack of access to health services and health insurance may be a contributing factor for the health disparity. Others feel that "having access is no guarantee that what you need is what you get. Furthermore, having insurance is no guarantee that the service that you receive is equal to that provided for your White Counterpart" (Collins 1996, p. 3). So, if 57 percent of African Americans have health insurance and 18 percent rely on Medicaid (Reed et al. 1993, p. 118) then where does the answer to poor health lie? I believe some of the blame rests with the effects of sexism, racism, poverty, miseducation, ageism, and all the other "isms." However, we African American women must take some responsibility for our health and do everything in our power to prevent any further deterioration in our health status. In part I of this book, you are shown how stress is a precursor to some illnesses that plague African American women. Lifestyle behaviors in most of the illnesses discussed are those that with the right intervention (i.e., eat less, no fried chicken wings, and reduce fat intake) African American women's health will improve. By showing you these stress-related illnesses, I hope that you will adjust your behaviors and reduce your stress in order to live a healthy life.

CHAPTER 1

The Impact of Stress: Does It Really Matter?

Shielding ourselves from the effects of stress is an important matter for African American women. To ascertain your stress level, please take a few minutes to complete the easy-to-score Stress Test Survey (Table 1.1). Please complete the survey now.

Each yes answer counts as one point and each no answer counts as zero. "The closer your yes total is to 58, the higher your stress index and the greater your need to employ some of the techniques discussed" (Slaby 1988, pp. 9–11) in part II of this book.

Now that you know what your stress level is, let's turn our attention to why it's important to know if you are falling victim to the effects of stress.

African American women's life expectancy is one indicator that tells us how well we are doing. Life expectancy not only tells us how long African American women are expected to live; it also serves as a good indicator of how they are meeting the challenges of society. In comparison to their white counterparts, as indicated in Table 1.2, it is apparent that African American women are not meeting those challenges very well.

Researchers believe that many diseases stem from stress, affecting our lives in a variety of ways. These stress-related diseases are discussed in part I, and ways to combat their effects are examined in part II. We must keep in mind, however, that many studies of stress-related illnesses were conducted with no African American women as research subjects. Only now are African American women seen as a very important variable in health-related research study design. Also worth noting is that many African American women are reluctant to participate in research. This is due partly to historical abuses like the federal government's experiments

Table 1.1
Stress Test Survey

Do you . . .	Yes	No
1. Ignore self-examination?	☐	☐
2. Drink lots of coffee?	☐	☐
3. Neglect vitamins?	☐	☐
4. Disregard salt intake?	☐	☐
5. Skip meals?	☐	☐
6. Do everything yourself?	☐	☐
7. Ignore others' suggestions?	☐	☐
8. Blow up?	☐	☐
9. Pursue unrealistic goals?	☐	☐
10. Lack a plan?	☐	☐
11. Not take time to relax your muscles?	☐	☐
12. Forget to laugh?	☐	☐
13. Act rude?	☐	☐
14. Not know your values?	☐	☐
15. Ignore your body's signals?	☐	☐
16. Deny reality?	☐	☐
17. Fail to test your stress tolerance?	☐	☐
18. Make a big deal out of a lot of things?	☐	☐
19. Discount meditation?	☐	☐
20. Let others seek things for you?	☐	☐
21. Have difficulty making decisions?	☐	☐
22. Lack knowledge of your strengths and weaknesses?	☐	☐
23. Lack organization?	☐	☐
24. Minimize encounters with people and ideas different from yours?	☐	☐
25. Avoid crises?	☐	☐
26. Keep everything inside?	☐	☐
27. Lack imagination?	☐	☐
28. Not belong to a support group?	☐	☐
29. Not exercise?	☐	☐
30. Lack interpersonal skills?	☐	☐
31. Not seek help for symptoms of stress?	☐	☐
32. Think yoga, zen, and self-hypnosis are silly?	☐	☐
33. Feel your life is out of control?	☐	☐
34. Fail to leave time for the unexpected?	☐	☐
35. Minimize rest?	☐	☐
36. Not remember when you were last massaged?	☐	☐
37. Not create buffer zones before and after anticipated stress?	☐	☐
38. Find yourself waiting for someone and getting angry?	☐	☐
39. Think everyone is replaceable?	☐	☐
40. Procrastinate?	☐	☐
41. Hide your weaknesses?	☐	☐
42. Find yourself spending a lot of time lamenting the past?	☐	☐
43. Not believe in the spiritual?	☐	☐
44. Find yourself unprepared?	☐	☐
45. Dress down?	☐	☐
46. Fail to build relaxation time into your schedule?	☐	☐
47. Have only one right way to do something?	☐	☐
48. Never let yourself go?	☐	☐
49. Say yes to everything?	☐	☐
50. Gossip?	☐	☐
51. Race through the day?	☐	☐
52. Not escape noise and people?	☐	☐
53. Abhor routine?	☐	☐
54. Fail to communicate roles?	☐	☐
55. Frequently encounter surprises?	☐	☐
56. Ignore how your office and house are arranged?	☐	☐
57. Not explore uses of new technologies in your life?	☐	☐
58. Let friends into your life?	☐	☐

Total _____

Table 1.2
White and Black Women's Life Expectancy

Race	1960	1970	1980	1990	1992	*1998
White	74.1	75.6	78.7	79.4	79.7	80.0
Black	66.3	68.3	72.5	73.6	73.9	74.8

Sources: Wegman (1990) 1960, 1979, 1980, Table 4, p. 841; Wegman (1993) 1990, 1992, 1993, Table 4, p. 747.

The Women's Health Data Book, (1995), Table 4.1, p. 65.

involving infecting Tuskegee men with syphilis and the sterilization of young African American women by health providers. These kinds of abuses left a residue of suspicions. For a more detailed discussion of this issue, see Collins (1996) "Commentary on the Health and Social Status of African American Women" (pp. 1–10). To illustrate how important the inclusion of African American women is to understanding the impact of stress on their health status, I will present research findings from as many studies as are available that incorporate African American women as subjects.

In the chapter that follows, I focus on the diseases that are most prevalent among African American women.

CHAPTER 2

Stress, Health, and the Body's Response

The physiological effects of stress and how the body responds to it are pertinent to the survival of African American women. This chapter is not meant to delve into the technical aspects of the immune response to stress, but rather to offer a brief look at African American women's diseases that may be stress related or have a stress component. The starting point for this discussion is the listing of ten leading causes of death among African American women (see Table 2.1). In studying the data in Table 2.1, we see that the number-one cause of death among both African American women

Table 2.1
Ten Leading Causes of Death among African/White American Women, 1999

Disease	African American Women	White American Women
1	Heart Disease	Heart Disease
2	Malignant Neoplasmas	Malignant Neoplasmas
3	Cerebrovascular Disease	Cerebrovascular Disease
4	Diabetes	Chronic Lower Respiratory Disease
5	Unintentional Injuries	Pneumonia/Influenza
6	Nephritis, Nephrotic Nephrosis Syndrome	Alzheimer's Disease
7	Chronic Lower Respiratory Disease	Unintentional Injuries
8	Septicemia	Diabetes
9	Influenza/Pneumonia	Nephritis, Nephrotic Nephrosis Syndrome
10	HIV Disease	Septicemia

Source: Health, United States 2001 With Urban & Rural Health Chartbook, (2001), Table 32, p. 177.

and white American women is heart disease. Women are dying of heart disease at an alarming rate, a rate that outnumbers deaths from cancer.

In the following pages I will present information on how your body responds to stress-induced illnesses and how symptoms of those illnesses may be relieved through the use of certain stress busters.

YOUR BODY'S RESPONSE TO STRESS

Bouchez (1994, p. 1) reported that the "number of black women dying from cardiovascular disease is nearly 70 percent higher than white women, [and] their risk of stroke is a whopping 80 percent higher." Most women believe that breast cancer kills more women than heart disease; however, each year 250,000 women die from heart attacks while 46,000 die from breast cancer (Dodd and Doner 2002, p. 53). As you can see from Table 2.2, for African American women mortality from heart disease increases with age and is highest among black females at all ages with the exception of those eighty-five and over.

The human heart is supported by a vascular system composed of 80,000 arteries and veins. This network supplies the heart with needed nourishment, like oxygenated blood and other substances. When these vessels are in good shape, blood flows smoothly, placing minimal stress on the heart. However, when we encounter stress, our heart, which normally beats 100,000 times a day, speeds up, sending blood rushing through our veins and arteries. Over long periods of stress, the vessel linings can wear down as blood rushes through them. Compounding and contributing to the strain placed on these vessels are African American women's diets that are high in fats that leave a residue of fatty deposits on the lining of the blood vessels making them narrow over time. When African American women encounter a stressful situation (such as racism), their heart rate increases and some of these fatty deposits may become dislodged and freely float until they reach a location where they are stopped. This causes a decrease in blood flow to the heart and makes the heart work harder. Over long

Table 2.2
Death Rates from Heart Disease for Women According to Age and Race in the United States (1989–1991) per 100,000 Population

Age (years)	White	Black
45-54	49.9	155.6
55-64	193.1	444.8
65-74	584.7	1,028.1
75-84	1,876.9	2,289.0
85	6,550.1	5,767.1

Source: Adapted from The Women's Health Data Book (1995), tables 3–4, p. 57.

periods when black women face a constant barrage of unpleasant events, the heart races and pumps harder because of the clogged blood vessels decreasing the flow of blood. This is one of the factors contributing to heart damage.

Very little cardiovascular research has been conducted with African American women as subjects. However, with the increasing death rate among these women, some researchers are now including them in studies focusing on this issue.

In one of these studies, Morris-Prather et al. (1996, p. 123) "examined the cardiovascular and emotional effects of realistic socially stressful events experienced by African American women." Fifty-two women were asked to view filmed vignettes of two stressful situations. One portrayed an unjust arrest for shoplifting and the other depicted an encounter with a rude and threatening highway patrolman. Each scene was counter-balanced with a white and/or a black perpetrator. After viewing the vignettes, the African American women in the study experienced an increase in tension and pulse rates because of what they had just seen. Often African American women suppress what they feel, which has harmful effects.

From this study you can see that certain encounters, like those involving racist behavior, can increase an individual's heart rate. Imagine how often African American women were bombarded with images of the Rodney King beating. Then imagine how fast their heartbeats must have increased, especially when the media and others attempted to convince them they hadn't witnessed this outrageous act or that it was justifiable.

Now turn your attention to the nationally televised account of an African American nurse in North Carolina who was pulled from her car by a state trooper, called names, and arrested because she did not recognize that he was a law enforcement officer in an unmarked police car and she was afraid of being carjacked. These are but a few examples of exposure to events that can increase your heart rate, causing fat deposits (accumulated from all of those fried chicken wings and macaroni & cheese) that float through narrow blood vessels and may precipitate a stroke or heart attack.

Some researchers have sought to identify the potential role of psychological and social factors in precipitating chest pain. In a study of 188 black women (Fisher et al. 1996, p. 30), 48 percent of participants reported significantly higher levels of stress prior to chest pain, as measured by the Perceived Stress Scale.

In another study (Maynard et al. 1995) of female patients who experienced myocardial infarction (a heart attack), Maynard and colleagues found that, compared to their white counterparts, African American women with a blood clot in the heart muscle who were admitted to a coronary-care unit were more likely to be younger, single, unemployed, and without health insurance. Furthermore, when adjusted for age, African American women were more likely to develop *acute* myocardial infarction and were more likely to die in the hospital (p. 339). Certainly, being unemployed and having no health insurance would be stressors for anyone, single or married.

STRESS: A PRECURSOR TO CANCER?

In the book *Managing Cancer* (2001, p. 4) Rawls and Lloyd state that "Cancer is particularly hard on black people [as indicated by] the overall incidence of Cancer in African Americans is 436.5% per 100,000, compared to 402.9% per 100,000 in White Americans." They go on to say that "Further, if this wasn't bad enough for breast cancer alone, each year more than 18,000 African American women will develop breast cancer and 5,000 will die from breast cancer" (p. 75). The incidence of cervical cancer among black females is 2.5 times higher than it is among white females, and lung cancer death rates continue to increase for both black and white females. Once African American women are diagnosed with any form of cancer, their survival rate lags far behind that of their white counterparts, with 63 percent of African American women survivors as opposed to 78 percent of white women. In 1988, 53,968 African Americans died from cancer and 23,647 of them were women (Scott 1993, p. 34). The most recent statistics from the American Cancer Society show that the cancer incidence rate for African Americans in 1994 was 454 per 100,000; for whites it was 394 per 100,000. Between 1990 and 1994, the incidence of cancer increased 1.2 percent for African Americans while decreasing 0.8 percent for whites (American Cancer Society 1998, p. 9).

What is causing the increase in cancer among African American women? More importantly, why are African American women's survival rates so poor? Research into causal factors have focused a lot of attention on genetic links, as well as behavioral and environmental factors. For African American people who are forced by America's social structure to endure so many hardships brought on by social factors such as racism, poverty, sexism, lack of education, segregation, and health/medical access issues, the role that stress plays or contributes to a poor prognosis must be considered. Since we know that psychological factors definitely influence the course of some illnesses, can we completely disregard the involvement of psychological factors in cancer?

As early as the nineteenth century, some researchers attempted to investigate the links between mind and body in disease. LeShane (1959), in his article "Psychological State as Factor in the Development of Malignant Diseases: A Critical Review," reported on one such researcher/physician, Nunn, who in a 1822 investigation emphasized that emotional factors influenced the growth of tumors of the breast. Nunn describes a woman with a "tumor of the right breast and nodules on the body . . . [on] the 18th of January 1813. A general shrinkage of the tumors to a most remarkable degree . . . this coincides with a shock to her nervous system caused by the death of her husband. Shortly thereafter the tumors again increased in size and the patient died" (LeShane 1959, p. 2). LeShane further reports on a study by Elida Evans who examined one hundred patients to determine the relationship between psychological factors and neoplasm/cancer growths. Evans reported, "The typical cancer patient had lost an important emotional relationship prior to the development of the neoplasm, and was unable to secure any effective outlet for his psychic energy. Under stress of the intense renunciation the detached energy had turned inward and, in expressing itself through a primitive erotic outlet, had brought the cancer into existence" (p. 6). Unfortunately, no research studies were found with African American women as subjects that probed stress and its relationship to the incidence of cancer. However, a study by Bacon et al. (1952), which investigated forty women with breast cancer using a psychological history–taking approach, looked at certain behavioral characteristics. The behavioral characteristics measured were "1. the masochistic character structure; 2. inhibited sexuality; 3. inhibited motherhood; 4. the inability to discharge or deal appropriately with anger, aggressiveness, or hostility, covered over by a façade of pleasantness; 5. the unresolved hostile conflict with mother, handled through denial and unrealistic sacrifices; and 6. a delay in securing treatment" (Bacon, Rennecker, and Kuther 1952, p. 454). It is worth a second look at number 4—"the inability to discharge anger or dealing appropriately with anger" —because of the racism and sexism that African American women are confronted with in the work environment. Although this study did not yield any concrete evidence to support what "triggers the change [from] cellular order to cellular chaos [cancer]," it did raise our awareness of a possible emotional link to cancer.

In another study of 160 women, Greer (1975) interviewed women the day before their breast biopsy for indicators of stressful life events. These interviews uncovered life events that caused depression, hostility, and other psychological variables, all of which were substantiated by a husband or other family member. The results of the biopsies were 69 breast cancers and 91 cases of benign breast disease. The investigator recognized that some controls were not in place—for example, there were no controls for the subjects' age, for what the doctor told each patient, or for the impact of fear. However, this study did recognize that there *may be* an emotional link to breast cancer.

In my quest to identify research evidence that supports psychological stress as a predictor of cancer, I found an interesting Danish study. From 1943 to 1985, the parents of children with cancer were followed to see if the psychological stress of the children's illness would lead to cancer in their parents. In the 11,231 parents identified from records in the Danish Cancer

Registry, 1,665 parental malignancies were diagnosed from the date the cancer was reported in their child (Johansen and Olsen 1997). Although this is a bit like backing into the possibility that stress may contribute to cancer development, the Johansen and Olsen study does provide some useful information upon which to continue the research. By no means are these studies conclusive; however, they raised the author's, and hopefully the reader's consciousness, about the importance of not taking personal stress lightly. Until cancer research conclusively shows the role of stress in the survival rates of African American women, they must control and shield themselves as much as possible from stressful events in their lives.

HYPERTENSION: ANOTHER SILENT KILLER

One in four African American women suffer from hypertension (high blood pressure) as compared to one in six white women. Hypertension is known by some as the "silent killer." Dr. Cynthia Crawford-Green (1996, p. 59) points out that the data is clear that "control of blood pressure (hypertension) can reduce the incidence of stroke. . . . " Further, Dr. Crawford-Green, a private practitioner who specializes in severe hypertension, states, "The cause of hypertension is unknown, but there is no doubt that stress, obesity and genetics . . . play contributing complex roles in the pathogenesis of hypertension" (p. 72). So what is a good blood pressure reading? There are many opinions: I believe that a reading of 120/60 is good and a reading of 140/90 or higher is not good. The aim of most practitioners is to keep blood pressure under control. Is that possible, especially when "everything from racism to soul food to genetics has been fingered in efforts to explain why hypertension is so prevalent among African Americans"? (Duhart 1996). And if racism is a factor, how do you control it?

One way to control hypertension is to change your lifestyle to buffer yourself from stressors. This may be easier said than done, since research points to suppressed hostility as a key source of stress, and racism in America promotes suppressed hostility in African Americans. Racism and major life crises and events—such as the death of a loved one, a divorce, or the loss of a job—may adversely impact health. Assuming that there is a relationship between daily hassles and health, then, African Americans are particularly at risk for poor health. African Americans' poor health status and shorter life expectancy lend credence to this assumption.

Derrick (1997) cites an example of how this plays out in one study. Derrick reports that "Duke University Medical Center had 30 healthy black women debate with a white [person] on two controversial topics, one of which was on race. When provoked with racist remarks, the women showed increased heart rates and blood pressure" (Derrick 1997, p. 37). As mentioned previously, when your heart beats faster, blood rushes through narrow blood vessels. And if fatty deposits, known as plaque, are dislodged by the force of the blood, they float through the bloodstream until they become lodged elsewhere, perhaps in the brain or the heart. Derrick also reported that racist remarks made during the debate prolonged the symptoms as opposed to remarks made during the debate on another topic. This study also supports my contention that the chronic stress of racism may be one reason why African Americans are twice as likely as whites to develop hypertension, as further noted by one of the Duke study's researchers. As noted previously, in addition to being twice as likely as whites to suffer from hypertension, African Americans tend to develop hypertension at an earlier age, and they are five times more likely to have severe hypertension and suffer more hypertension-related complications, such as stroke (Keller, Fleury, and Bergstrom 1995).

African American women like Cathy Collins, a wife, mother, and a member of Jack and Jill of America, Inc. participated in a study that was reported by Tierney (1988) in a *New York Times* article "Wired for Stress." Mrs. Collins allowed herself to be monitored for twenty-four hours by an electrical device strapped to her waist that recorded her blood pressure and pulse. When her boss approached her with a sheet of paper and said, "Cathy, I need this Xeroxed right away, please," a beep sounded. At that moment, the machine around her waist started drawing in air, and the blood pressure cuff on her arm tightened. The monitor showed that her pulse, which had been 71, had risen to 82. Her blood pressure was 116/72. In this case, 72 (which is used to diagnose hypertension, which measures pressure between heart beats) had risen 26 percent (Tierney 1988, p. 48).

Now, just imagine how many times a day someone in your surroundings asks you to do something that stresses you out or just imagine that you are on your way home from work and you stop by the local food store. You walk up to the counter. Patiently, you wait your turn. You note that the person behind the counter is waiting on the only other person beside yourself. Now another customer, a white woman, walks up to the counter. You immediately know that you are going to have to defend your position of "next in line" to be waited on. Of course, as with Mrs. Collins, your pulse rate begins to increase and you say to yourself, "Not today." As the clerk finishes waiting on the previous customer and asks, "Who's next?" this makes your heart race even more because the clerk (a white male) knew that you were there when he began to help the other customer and you are still there now. Obviously, he never expected you to speak up and say in a loud, authoritative voice, "I'm next." This has happened to me on so many occasions, I have lost count. Do these encounters increase your heart rate and impact your health? Yes, they do. Especially if you don't deal with them when they happen (as I have) and the incident is stored in the worry section of your brain. These continued uncontrollable stressors may "eventually contribute to permanent high blood pressure as well as to other afflictions—stroke, arteriosclerosis, heart attack" (Tierney 1988, p. 47).

RESPONSES TO STRESS BY THE MIND AND THE REPRODUCTIVE SYSTEM

As women, sometimes we experience disruptions in our menstrual cycle, our reproductive health, and our sex drive. Certain hormones play an active role in controlling these bodily functions. The body works like this: the brain releases two key hormones, Luteinizing Hormone Releasing Hormone (LHRH), and Follicle-Stimulating Hormone (FSH). These hormones stimulate the ovaries to release eggs, estrogen, and progesterone to perform specific functions. When you experience stress, two brain chemicals—endorphins and enkephalins—are affected and they, in turn, inhibit the hypothalamus gland in the brain from releasing LHRH. This one event interferes with the timely release of other hormones, and your endocrine system is now out of balance. For example, two weeks before your menstrual cycle, when your child comes home from school and tells you the assistant principal's son called him a nigger (true story), expect your menstrual cycle and sex drive to be affected at least until you resolve the problem. When women are under stress, estrogen secretion is suppressed. Therefore, what it stimulates—the sex drive and the menstrual cycle—is also affected.

During the reign of the Nazis in Germany, 54 percent of Jewish women of childbearing age stopped menstruating within their first months in concentration camps because of the stress brought on by the threat of extermination. What is important to know is that "a variety of hormones secreted by the hypothalamus in the brain, the pituitary gland and the adrenal glands bind to cells of the immune system and alter their functions" (Edlin, Golanty, and Brown 1996, p. 51).

THE AFRICAN AMERICAN FEMALE'S IMMUNE RESPONSE TO STRESS: OBESITY, STDS, DIABETES, DEPRESSION, AND SUICIDE

The immune system is one of the body's major defenses against foreign invaders. Like the skin, the immune system attempts to keep us well by keeping invaders out or under control, thus maintaining homeostasis. When our immune system is fully armed, we stay well. When our defenses are down, we are susceptible to various illnesses. The functioning of the immune system, with all its specialized attack cells—for example, T4 cells in the fight against the HIV virus—is beyond the scope of this discussion. However, in African American women, some familiar diseases, like Type II diabetes, herpes, yeast infections, rheumatoid arthritis, and common colds/influenza, will be discussed, as well as depression and its ultimate expression, suicide.

The American Diabetes Association estimates that there are 3 million African Americans who suffer from diabetes mellitus. More specifically, among African American women, diabetes is the fourth leading cause of death. Diabetes is characterized by the pancreas' inability to produce enough insulin to regulate the amount of sugar ingested. Diabetes is so prevalent among African American women that causal factors are important to their very survival.

Obesity appears to be one of the precipitating factors in the development of Type II diabetes. Obesity in African American women is a critical issue because obesity is not only twice as prevalent among black women as it is among white women but also a precursor of hypertension as well as diabetes.

With a sedentary lifestyle that lacks an established exercise program and with diets laced with high fat and low in fiber "60 percent of our sisters become obese by middle age when we should be cautiously addressing all of our inappropriate health care habits" (Johnson 1996, p. 10). For example, Walcott-McQuigg (1995) studied middle-aged women's psychosocial weight-control behavior. Both Johnson and Walcott-McQuigg found from their analysis of responses to the Global Stress Scale that women who were overweight were experiencing more stress than those who were not overweight, and 50 percent of the women thought stress brought on their weight gain. Therefore, when overweight African American women experience some form of stress, the body responds in various ways. What is important for us to recognize is that stress can trigger certain bodily responses that create and exacerbate adverse health conditions.

For example, a 1963 study by Slawson, Flynn, and Kollar found that when twenty-five newly diagnosed diabetics took the Minnesota Multiphasic Personality Inventory, the subjects had experienced some type of stress prior to the onset of the disease. Half of the study's subjects had experienced the death of a loved one and bereavement or some other loss/separation, and one-quarter had experienced some minor loss. Another study found that within a year of the onset of diabetes, 74 percent of the subjects reported that stressful events had occurred at work or at home (Kisch 1985).

Turning our attention to sexually transmitted diseases (STDs), it is estimated that each year 40 million sexually transmitted viral infections will affect the American population, among them 30 million cases of herpes. Herpes Simplex Virus Type 2 (HSV2) is a highly infectious virus that appears in the genital areas as lesions. These lesions reappear in response to psychological stress, according to numerous studies (Bonneau, 1994; Learum et al., 1991; Longo and Clum, 1989; Schmidt, 1985; Stout and

Bloom, 1986). The emotional stresses that African Americans experience require the utmost attention for women affected by HSV2. Evidence is clear (Learum et al., 1991) that emotional stress triggers flare-ups of this lifelong chronic infectious condition, and racism is at the top of the list of stressors for African Americans. Controlling the condition requires a stringent regimen of mind-altering exercises. Regarding the impact of stress on African American women with HSV2, one study of the recurrent herpes virus (cold sore) found that among 61 student nurses who had experienced certain life changes that altered their mood, 14 percent had a recurrence (Katcher et al. 1973). Friedman, Katcher, and Brightman (1977), in their study of 149 nurses who experienced negative mood swings, found that they, too, also had a recurrence of the herpes virus (cold sore).

Another illness that attacks young and old alike and that hampers their quality of life is rheumatoid arthritis, a chronic inflammatory disease that causes painful swollen joints. According to Horton (1995, p. 70), who reported on rheumatoid arthritis, "Women are two to three times more affected than men." Although Horton reports "that there is no significant difference in the incidence of rheumatoid arthritis between blacks and whites . . . the disease is much more severe in those of lower socioeconomic status" (Horton 1995, p. 70). Because many African American women live below the poverty level, they are at particular risk. Furthermore, there is evidence that before the flare-up of the disease, people generally experience some form of abrupt life event (e.g., the loss of a spouse) or another unpleasant event (Whitcare, Cummings, and Griffin 1994, p. 78). As noted previously, stress brought on by racism cannot be ignored.

The ever-increasing demands on African American women can lead to depression. Bertram-Brooks (1996, p. 108) notes, "In general depression is viewed as an affective disorder characterized by disturbances of mood. It includes negative perceptions of self such as self-blame, self-degradation, unworthiness, helplessness, and hopelessness. Not infrequently, it includes thoughts of death or suicide." We now turn to the issue of suicide. However, approximately 7 million women suffer from diagnosable major depression, the precursor to the act. Women make 2 million annual visits to mental health professionals, and depression occurs more frequently in women twenty-five to forty-four years of age (Horton 1995). Due to the positions they hold in their family and community, women tend to place themselves in the line of fire for all kinds of stressful events. Bertram-Brooks's (1996) review of the literature regarding African American women and depression notes that there is a paucity of studies dealing with this illness. However, she reports on those relevant to African American women, citing Barbie (1992) and Worthington (1992) as most noteworthy in their attempts to ferret out the relevant literature. I turn your attention to a much more thorough discussion of depression found in their research. Of particular interest to this discussion are African American women who are burdened with the experiences of racism, classism, sexism, and poverty, which puts them at considerable risk for the ultimate expression of depression—suicide.

It has been a very long-standing myth that African American women do not commit suicide. Although they are less likely to commit suicide than white women African American women are still vulnerable. (In 1998 there were 5,474 suicides committed by white women as opposed to 318 suicides committed by black women. In 1999 there were 5,193 suicides by white women as opposed to 299 by black women.) The vulnerability of African American women to suicide stems from their "Jinks So" position in society. This rings true in the case of journalist Leonita McClain, who at thirty-one ended her own life. Accounts of her life show her to have been a talented African American woman who probably had to defend her scholarly accomplishments and abilities every day of her life. As Starling (1999, p. 143) reported, "The devastating effect of depression is not new. As far back as actress Dorothy Dandridge—and more recently songstress Phyllis Hyman, Chicago columnist Leanita McClain, author Terri Jewell and Pittsburgh executive Dianna Green—Black women lost in depression have committed suicide" and were taking the so-called easy way—overdosing on pills. Dianna Green "took a .22 caliber silver pistol—and with her Bible by her side—pulled the trigger, killing herself with a single shot to the head" (Weathers 1998, p. 82). In the case of two of my friends—one put a shotgun in her mouth and the other took pills—depression preceded both their suicides.

Like so many others, the daily struggles just to do the job you are paid to do can be overwhelming. You see, while some of us in our early years learn to shield ourselves from the negative barrage to our character, others are not so lucky. Like the character Velma in Toni Cade Bambara's book *The Salt Eaters,* who contemplated suicide and followed through on the voice that told her "It's better on the other side," they simply wear out and commit suicide out of desperation. We must be ever mindful that depression must be controlled. Starling (1999) also lists warning signs of depression and suggests that if you have five or more of these signs for at least two weeks you should see a doctor:

- Dramatic weight loss
- Insomnia (sleeping too little) or hypersomnia (sleeping too much)
- Trouble concentrating
- Loss of energy, sluggishness
- Extreme feelings of sadness
- Feelings of guilt and worthlessness
- Recurrent thoughts of death
- Slowed or agitated physical/speaking response

- Unexplained physical ailments
- Little interest in formerly pleasurable pastimes or sex

How we approach these symptoms of stress will be discussed later within the context of relationships in our family, at work, and in our community.

CHAPTER 3

Managing Stress at Home

On a daily basis, the American public is bombarded with negative images of the African American family. When the nightly news reports on welfare reform, the images that are broadcast usually show an African American female who is single with four children living in squalor. By contrast, when reporters show a white female welfare recipient who is also single with four children, most of the time we learn that she just got off welfare and is working to support her children. Images like these—showing black single mothers mired in poverty, while white single mothers are raising themselves up by their bootstraps—are generalized by the American public to be descriptive of the typical families in the African American community. What is lacking on the nightly news or other similar television programs are images of stable, two-parent, professional African American families like the Huxtables (Bill Cosby's TV family) or those found in the membership of Jack and Jill of America, Inc. (discussed in part II). Also lacking is a historical foundation that would help the public better understand why some African American families have problems. African American families are particularly vulnerable because of social forces that impact their lives—racism, unemployment, lack of a proper education, lack of health insurance, sexism, and poverty. Having a better understanding of how situations like these and many others develop in our nation may help erase some of the negative myths about African American families. A comprehensive historical overview of these and other social factors affecting African American family life is beyond the scope of this chapter. However, this chapter does offer a contextual framework, which demonstrates the insurmountable stress that African American

families face each day, in the hope that all readers will gain a better understanding of the impact life stresses have on family life.

THE IMPACT OF SLAVERY ON THE AFRICAN
AMERICAN FAMILY: THE TRUTHS AND UNTRUTHS

Historically, the experiences of slavery did have an effect on the African
female slaves. White male slave masters forced slave women to have
babies by any male slave they owned, then they separated them from their
babies and children, selling the children to the highest bidder and, yes,
forbidding the couple from marrying. In spite of this bondage, which pro-
hibited the formation of a sound, stable family while the slavery system
was in force, some male slaves took a slave wife (to whom they were faith-
ful within the confines of white male sexual exploitation). Each of these
male slaves who took a female slave for a wife lived on another plantation
so he would not witness the sexual exploitation and inhumane treatment
his wife would receive at the hands of her white slave master. Even those
spoken for who lived on other plantations were not out of reach of the
vicious white slave master. In fact, "one study of marriages between
slaves in Tennessee, Louisiana and Mississippi found that from 1864 to
1866, almost one-third were broken up by the [white slave] master"
(Coontz 1992, p. 238).

Yet, as you can see, the slaves attempted to maintain some type of family bond through bondage. Frazier wrote (as reported in Taylor 1994,
p. 20) in his book "that slavery destroyed any familial structure" and laid
the groundwork for what we see in the dysfunctional family that is
headed by young black unmarried females. Further, Frazier posits that
slavery also provided the framework for the shift from the patriarchal to
the matriarchal unit.

Certainly there are other factors that Frazier missed. Ronald Taylor
(1994, p. 20) states, "Frazier's . . . important insight regarding the link
between family structure and economic resources was obscured by the
inordinate emphasis he placed on the instability and 'self-perpetuating
pathologies of lower class black families.' " Stability was something that
slaves desperately wanted and searched for. To discount the notion that
slavery was the culprit in the demise of the African American family is
unfounded. If that were the case, why, then, following the Emancipation
Proclamation, did slaves use the Freedman's Bureau to try to find their
mates from whom they had been separated through slavery? (Franklin
1988, p. 24). When this approach failed to locate loved ones, many freed
slaves traveled to other locations—some couples were united, but many
were not. In fact, the historian Herbert Gutman (1975) documents in his
research that "between 1855–1880, 70 percent to 90 percent of African
American households contained two parents, and 70 percent were

nuclear. . . . [B]y 1866, 9,452 former slaves from 17 countries, registered their marriages by entering their names in the marriage records and paid a 25-cent fee" (Franklin 1988, p. 24). This drive for kinship unification incensed former slave masters who missed, longed for, and needed free slave labor. Therefore, they did everything to keep families separated from their kin by passing laws designed to keep loved ones apart. One of these laws, the "apprentice law," was established to limit parental rights of African American slave children, thus preventing the family unit from staying together (Coontz 1992, p. 239). This, however, did not stop those who were newly freed and who still remembered how they had lived in the Motherland. This drive by newly freed slaves to maintain family ties was legitimized by the traditional American marriage; some actually participated in religious ceremonies. These African slaves were held in bondage—even after slavery was outlawed—while the white American family built a successful, strong family unit, supported by an educational system, a society that welcomed them, and an economic base that employed them. While white Americans built America, as they wanted it to work for them and their needs, they built a solid family foundation to reap the benefits of slave labor, and African American families began to weaken under the pressures of racism and economic oppression. Further, while African American women raised their master's children, assuming the title of the "other mother," they fed, cleaned, and sometimes breast-fed the master's children, all at the expense and neglect of their own children. By the end of the nineteenth century (between 1855 and 1905), across this nation African Americans were driven out of skilled jobs. African Americans have always been hit harder during economic downturns than other immigrants, especially those who immigrated from Ireland, Germany, and other European countries. When the head of the household is driven away, the entire family suffers. Some families survived intact; others did not.

Surviving life on the plantation, Reconstruction, and the Industrial Revolution, the African American family did not begin to experience a decline in the traditional two-family home until the 1960s, "when 75 percent of black households with children under the age of eighteen included both a husband and a wife" (Coontz 1992, p. 241). The structure of white families was also affected but, of course, not to the extent of African American families because white Americans' social and economic base supported their needs. When you are faced with racism and other social ills that prevent a family member (male) from acquiring the necessary skills to support his family, the results are broken and stressed families. African American families that were once held together by resources from their farmwork and a growing industrial base supported by a world war, began to fall apart under the pressure of the 1960s social bondage. In the 1960s, the so-called Second Emancipation and the passage of the Civil Rights Act supposedly freed African Americans from the oppression of segregation. Some felt that conditions would begin to change. It was at that time that the public began to hear criticism, which continues to this day, about social programs that destroyed the black family.

This argument is similar to that made by the late Daniel Patrick Moynihan, a U.S. senator, in his report "The Negro Family: The Case for National Action" (1965). In the study, Moynihan states that the "weakness in black family structure were identified as a major source of social problems in the black communities." The "Moynihan Report" as it came to be known, "attributed high rates of welfare dependency, out of wedlock births, educational failure, drug addiction, and other problems to the 'unnatural' dominance of women in the family" (Taylor 1997 p. 20). I do not wish to devote this chapter to attacking Senator Moynihan's report; that has been done by many other scholars. But there is a certain sense of pride that was, and still is, a very important aspect of self-love among white males; this is often reflected in their inability to accept any part of the blame, especially when they have had (or their ancestors have had) a hand in the wrongdoings. So they choose to omit the impact of segregation and slavery from their life and thinking. The social bondage of African Americans was exacerbated by white Americans who used a system of separation and segregation to distinguish the haves from the have-nots in a social structure that relied on racism and social policies to control the destiny of millions of African Americans. Researcher and educator Judy Katz (1978, p. 43), in her book *White Awareness,* states that "The problem in America isn't a black problem. It is essentially a white problem in that it is whites who developed it, perpetuated it and have the power to resolve it." Therefore, the ball is in their court and we are waiting for the game and the solution to begin. In fact, I assumed the events of September 11, 2001, would bring this nation's racial divisiveness to a halt, and in some cities across the country it did, for a moment. But I've begun to hear and see the same racist behavior beginning to resurface. However, I'm still hopeful.

The African American family survived in the 1970s and 1980s with the help of a social support system that encouraged the pooling of resources to save families with a kinship network. This pooling of resources allowed the mother to work while more and more European immigrants replaced her husband on the job. The lack of opportunities in America—stemming in part from white racism, discriminatory social welfare policies, and an emerging criminal justice system that incarcerated a disproportionately high number of black males—apparently helped to facilitate the rise in the African American matriarchy. In addition to racism, the family was besieged with another social ill of the 1970s and 1980s—the presence of drugs that fueled neighborhood violence and black-on-black crimes. The immediate effects of the antipoverty programs could not erase the historical ills plaguing African American lives and continued high unemployment for males.

African American families were facing the remnants of the preceding eras as they entered the twenty-first century. They brought with them the legacy of slavery, unprecedented poverty, high rates of separation and divorce, high infant mortality, high drug and alcohol abuse, a high rate of out-of-wedlock births, rising high school dropout rates, a high rate of community violence, high unemployment, and a high rate of incarceration of black males and females. If, in fact, we go through another century with the ills of the last four hundred years, the stress levels of African American families will certainly continue to rise and will be fatal unless there is some form of intervention from a variety of sources. However, because of the 9/11 terrorist attacks coupled with the Iraqi War of 2003, which has already cost 20 billion with an additional 2 billion a month to the end of 2003, there reportedly will be a loss of 1.6 million jobs in 2002; African American families must prepare for the stress that will surely have a tremendous impact on their lives.

AFRICAN AMERICAN FAMILY STRESS IN CONTEMPORARY AMERICA

Family stressors manifest themselves primarily in two areas: relationships and economics. While there may be others, stress appears to emanate mostly from these two issues. African American women must be aware of the sources of family stress so they can develop the buffers or coping behaviors that will protect their health.

Relationships and Economic Factors as Family Stressors

Family stressors are those that develop as a result of relationships among family members: mother, father, and children. To a lesser degree, extended family members can also be sources of stress; for example, the nagging mother-in law or the nosey and controlling sister-in-law. Stress from extended family members will not be included in this discussion; however, some of the de-stressors found throughout this book (like the use of caller ID) can make your life much easier when you do encounter their wrath. In a home where there is a mother and a father, the sources of stress may be very different than in a single female–headed home where the male presence may be sporadic and may periodically change. The father/husband who returns home each evening from his stable nine-to-five job may bring far less stress to the home environment than an unemployed boyfriend who visits on your payday or when she receives her monthly allotment from the government. Sometimes, even stable families are confronted with the erosion of the failing American economy. With an unstable economy, the two-income family structure has emerged. As previously mentioned, the war with Iraq has resulted in an increased cost for national security. This, coupled with the first wave of welfare reform recipients to be eliminated from the welfare rolls, may prove fatal to some already shaky families and will make the two-income structure even more crucial. With the mother being forced out of the African American home to work, she assumes *another job* whereas most males have *just one job*. Along with her family chores, she must now delay washing the clothes until the weekend or the evening. After she has cooked, washed the dishes, helped with homework, reminded the kids to brush their teeth, laid out school clothes, rolled her hair, gotten her own clothing laid out for the next day, then she is expected to be the loving wife when she finally goes to bed. If she does not fulfill these obligations, the stress of these relationships is strained. Stress can emerge at any point where she must perform as mother, wife, or employee. Because a mother does spend more time with her children, she is usually the enforcer of family rules and the person who will reprimand the offenders. Resolving family conflict places the African American mom in the forefront of the conflict. How she manages this stress will certainly have an impact on her health status.

The idealized family (stay-at-home mom, father who works) is not always possible for the African American family. As Susan Toliver (1998, p. 4) states, "Because black families are concentrated in the lower two-fifths of US families, generally they have gained comparatively little. Among employed blacks, blacks families earn only 55% of what white families earn. Although more black families have attained middle-class status than ever before, their numbers still equal only one third of all black families." The shift in the economy—with married, childbearing women participating more and more in the workforce (Hartman 1989) and with nearly two-thirds of jobs since 1995 created for women in the service industry—will continue to impact family environments with overworked and busy moms. Without economic security for a family, exacerbated by poor wages, the climate is set for marital conflict, which may precipitate separation and divorce. This was substantiated by a Taylor (1994, p. 27) study that showed that "since the 1960s a sharp decline has occurred in the years black women spend with their first husband and a corresponding rise in the eventual separation and divorce between first and second marriages."

As a result, large numbers of African American women who have raised their children alone are now being left with the responsibility of raising their children's children. Burton (1992) studied how African American grandparents were coping with a second wave of children, becoming surrogate parents at a time when their health might be compromised by chronic medical conditions, resulting in a much shorter life span. Some of the stressors that African American grandmothers identified in the study stemmed from contextual, family, and individual issues. Some of the family stressors manifested themselves physically through illness, and psychologically through depression, anxiety, alcoholism, and increased smoking (Burton 1992, p. 750). Although these findings focused on elderly African American grandparents, they nevertheless have implications for any African American female who may be in a similar situation, such as taking care of an elderly mother with dementia or Alzheimer's or caring for a husband who has been diagnosed with prostate cancer.

STRESS IN MALE-FEMALE RELATIONSHIPS

African American males and females are under extraordinary economic and social pressures that place great strains on their marital relationship. As a result, there is a need to satisfy each other's needs for love and emotional support, but external factors out of their immediate control often interfere with the expression of love and the kind of emotional support they would like to extend. Because the "unemployment rate and welfare system combined to push black men from the center to the periphery, black men have been made transitory family members, that is to say, they have been made absent fathers, boyfriends, uncles and stepfathers who live on the margins of the female centered household network" (Staples 1991, p. 202). When one of these absent males feels compelled to visit his ex-wife or girlfriend, he encounters stressors associated with her need for love and affection or the kids' needs for school clothes. If he's unemployed, this absent male feels as if his own stress from his perceived failures in life is compounded by the disappointment expressed by the family he sees so infrequently, so he simply stays away. The female interprets his absence as a sign that he doesn't care, which causes her to feel a deep sense of loneliness and despair. Some of these women turn to substances like alcohol to help relieve their stress, but this only opens the door to an even greater stressor.

For African American females who live with their husbands, similar stressors may be at work. As mentioned previously, economic pressure is one of the major sources of stress in a family. If the husband works, he is then exposed to related stresses that will have an impact on his marital relationship. How the female homemaker addresses her husband's work-related stress will also have a ripple effect on her children's lives if not handled appropriately. Women feel they must be responsible for the outcome of their relationship with their husband. Some women will take abuse and other unpleasant behavior to keep peace in a relationship. In her book *The Best Kind of Loving*, Dr. Gwendolyn Grant Goldsby (1995) presents the story of Kit who took long-term abuse—from verbally abusive name calling, such as "Black Bitch," to physical abuse, including a broken arm. She was abused on one occasion because she did not stop watering the plants to listen to what her male partner had to say (Grant Goldsby 1995, p. 106). A woman who believes the abusive man is the only male who can make her happy may accept his long-term abuse. These are relationships filled with stress, often resulting in separation and divorce. As Dr. Grant Goldsby points out, drugs and alcohol may be involved, but this is no excuse to hit, beat, and sometimes murder. Stress that is associated with family violence is beyond the scope of this discussion. However, there are many agencies that can be contacted for assistance. The national hot line for domestic abuse (1-800-799-7233) or local social service agencies are available to assist you.

There are, however, those marital relationships that are protected by the African American female from stressors both external (racism) and internal (work overload). Some couples may take time out to strengthen their relationship. Some couples who seriously want their marriage to work and want to control stress may:

- Have weekly meetings to keep tension under control in the household.
- Establish a travel schedule for mom and dad with no kids allowed (a week alone or a weekend).
- Set aside one day a week for quiet, uninterrupted time alone (bedroom becomes off-limits for children).
- Have lunch together once every ten days.
- Select books and articles for each other that have relevance to the marriage.
- Keep wedding albums on the bedroom shelf, not hidden away. Remember this was an event that made both of you very happy.
- Set budget goals. Money and income can be a source of continuous family/marital stress.

African American marital relationships, as previously mentioned, are under such extraordinary economic and social pressures that many do not survive. The reaffirmation of the marriage commitment must be kept in the forefront when life stressors seem to overshadow love and devotion.

CHILDREN AND THE STRESS THEY CAUSE

Children can be sources of stress for their parents, especially the mother. Because she spends the majority of her time with the children, the African American woman must understand her children's sources of stress so she can better address their needs.

Dr. Archibald Hart (1992), in his book *Stress and Your Children*, identifies specific stress issues that children may encounter at various stages of development. I have selected some of these sources of stress for presentation here, followed by a brief discussion about how to approach them in an effort to control your stress levels (Hart 1992, p. 63).

Stress Issues for Preadolescents (Age Nine to Thirteen)
Self-consciousness over physical signs of development.

Increased concern over social pressures and acceptance.

Confusion about sex roles and opposite sex.

Concerns about overdevelopment or underdevelopment.

Intense introspection.

Conflict with parents over amount of freedom.

Testing of boundaries by rebelling.

Continuing pressure about drugs and sex.

Stress Issues for Early Adolescents (Age Twelve to Fourteen)
Intense group pressure and the need to belong.

Entry into high school environment.

Testing boundaries of control.

Dating issues and sexual pressures; ongoing drug pressures.

Acute self-esteem issues.

Stress Issues for Older Adolescents (Age Fourteen through Sixteen)
Conflicts over desire for independence.

Increased financial pressures, e.g. clothes, car and CDs.

Peer pressure.

Disappointed over not achieving ideal self.

Experimentation with drugs and sex.

Continuing belongingness issues.

Growing sense of reality about who s/he really is.

Worry about future, education and marriage.

For African American children, understanding racism and why they are treated differently than white children will be discussed later in this chapter.

Stress for children can be brought on by school and peers. At-home relationships between children, parents, and siblings can be a source of great stress in a child's life as well. Home is the sanctuary for a child; however, with changing family structures due to high separation and divorce rates, compounded by remarriage that may result in blended families, children lose or must share their sanctuary.

Other family crises—like unemployment, alcoholism/drug use, Grandma coming to live with the family, illness of a parent, overcrowding, and sibling conflict—all increase the stress for the African American female. When her children bring home problems from school, which may be another source of their stress, she must help to alleviate their problems. One example that African American children face in public school is that many believe the public education system has given up on them. If they are in private school, they are isolated from those who look like them and a subtle type of racism may rear its ugly head. For example, the teacher in math honors class gives your son a poor grade on his math exam because he did not show all the steps in solving the problems, even though he came up with the correct answer, or the high school teacher may attempt to justify slavery, or the college president may give an address on Martin Luther King Day praising Abraham Lincoln for all the work he did to free the slaves.

Here's one example of how racism may play out in a private school setting: a teacher returns the math exams taken by the class. She then calls the only African American student in the class to the front of the classroom. The young African American male student assumes that he is going to be praised for his outstanding grade on the math test. However, the teacher points to him and says to the class, "How could you let him get a higher grade than you"?

And here's another private school situation: an African American male wrestler in an all-boys' private school is walking back to the gym from the water fountain, when a white male in a very low voice says the "N" word. When the African American male approaches the white male and asks, "What did you say?" the white male refuses to repeat what he said. However, another white male, also standing in the hallway next to the perpetrator, says, "I will not repeat it." The white male who made the statement is the son of the school's assistant principal.

And consider this public school situation: Danielle was sent to the principal's office by her Spanish teacher "for allegedly making a verbal protest when told to use Abraham Lincoln as a subject matter for Black History [month]" (Stevenson 1999, p. 3). Reportedly, things got worse once Danielle reached the office of the principal, Ms. Vitagliano. Danielle, who learned much of her black history at home, explained that she was well aware of Abraham Lincoln and the Emancipation, but felt they could learn about it another time. Reportedly, Vitagliano then responded, "You should be grateful for him because if it wasn't for him, y'all would still be picking cotton" (Stevenson 1999, p. 3).

Each day, in some of America's classrooms, African American children are exposed to overt and covert acts of racism. In addition to racism, there are other stressors in a student's life, including:

- Grades
- Tests
- An indifferent school system
- Crime
- Bullies
- Violence

- Theft of personal items
- Nonsupportive teachers
- Old textbooks
- Poor, deteriorating school buildings
- Lack of extracurricular activities

All these, and many more, are sources of stress for the child, mother, and family. When children come home after having endured personal attacks and other problems, African American women must find a way to defuse their anger, as well as a way to de-stress themselves.

SIBLINGS, PARENTS, PEERS, AND STRESS

Within the adolescent's environment, sibling(s), parents, and peers are the most important forces the adolescent must contend with. Each of these interactions may result in some form of conflict. Interaction between siblings may generate unbelievable stress for the entire family and, more specifically, the mother. In addition, "There is also evidence that birth order may affect a child's vulnerability to stress. In some ways, first born children tend to be more vulnerable" (Hart 1992, p. 61), not only because of their parents' expectations of them, but also because the parents may rely on them to be the leader or role model for the other siblings. Because the parents focus so much attention on the firstborn, the other sibling(s) may rebel against this sibling. Also, the middle child may feel left out or forgotten while the youngest may feel that he or she is forgotten, or may lash out at the other siblings. The African American mother may find herself in the middle of sibling squabbles morning, noon, and night. She must be prepared to resolve these conflicts to keep her own stress levels down. What's important is for the African American mother to recognize how she can best control her children's conflicts.

She must control the family environment by creating a structure that is flexible, yet limits stress-provoking incidents. For instance, she must treat all her children equally. Sometimes mothers tend to favor one child over another. This favoritism may come from a mother's recognition that one child may need more attention or that one child is the weakest. If the other siblings fail to recognize these weaknesses, they may grow to resent their sister or brother or will turn their resentment inward, creating internal stress for themselves.

What all this means to the African American mother is that she must not only understand how stress affects her health status, she must also understand the differences among her children and establish an environment that will be stress free. In my hometown in upstate New York, winters were very long. My mother understood how cabin fever would affect us and she taught us to play cards and checkers. When we got bored with these activities, she would put some music on and dance with us. When we got tired of dancing, she would sing religious songs to us. As mothers, we must become creative when conflict starts to erupt. By controlling our children's conflicts, we control our own stress levels. As in the following example, Mrs. Sara Johnson was very creative when it came to controlling her children's conflicts and her own stress level.

Mrs. Johnson, a stay-at-home mom who on rare occasions works from home as a lawyer, has a stress-busting practice worth mentioning. She reported to me that when she experiences any type of inappropriate behavior from her two sons, she pulls out her journal and writes down what has happened. When the journal is full, she literally shuts down. This means that she puts on her nightgown and robe and lies down on the sofa with a box of chocolate bon-bons and a good book. For twenty-four hours, she cooks no food, does no dishes, does no chauffeuring to sports practice, washes no favorite T-shirts, handles no wifely duties—nothing involving the family that takes her away from the sofa (except trips to the bathroom). In other words, *Don't call me. I'll call you.* What this does is reduce her stress and make her family appreciate her. When the twenty-four hours are over, she tosses the journal out and replaces it with a new one. When she resumes her mother/wife role and inappropriate behavior starts again, she only has to go near the journal and things quickly straighten out.

Controlling our children's sibling conflicts does not guarantee that we will not experience other relationship stressors. In fact, our parental role may become strained when we have disagreements with our children. These disagreements may arise from the adolescent's fight for independence, failure to complete home chores, unacceptable dress, personal hygiene issues, failure to meet school requirements, or improper use of family property (such as the car). Mothers spend more time with their children than fathers and generally enforce the rules and determine the punishment children will receive. Therefore, mothers are more likely to bear the brunt of the anger and resulting stress. This is particularly problematic for single females who are heads of households, where the mother must continually exert her parental authority. Unlike the married African American female, who may get some help from her husband in handing out punishment, the single female must impose all punishment and handle all authority issues.

Peers also create stress for one another, and the spillover may spread through a family, causing stress for all who encounter it. Parents must understand their children's sources of stress in the environment. As the Iverson and Scheer (1987) model in Figure 3.1 shows, parental influence is the most influential from grade 1 through grade 5. By sixth grade, as the model indicates, peers become extremely influential and may become a source of stress in the adolescent's life.

Figure 3.1
Changing Social Forces Concurrent with the Development of the Child

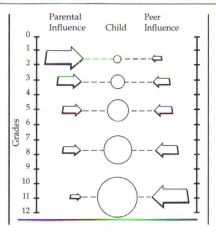

Source: Iverson and Scheer (1987), *Changing Social Forces Concurrent with the Development of the Child,* p. 27.

Collins (1990) tested the Iverson/Scheer model on first- to third-graders with the theoretical assumptions that parents exert the most influences during grade 1 to grade 6. Collins found that the children were most likely to be influenced by their parents during grade 1 to grade 3, and this is consistent with the Iverson and Scheer model (Collins 1990, p. 144). It is this peer influence (peer pressure from grades 5 and above, which the Iverson/Scheer model supports) that a parent must recognize as a potential source of stress, as well as other physiological stresses from colds, earaches, or viruses, and psychological stresses, from a boyfriend's or girlfriend's rejection, from failing grades, or from tension from ethical problems such as lying, sinfulness, and moral or sexual issues. An African American mother must also be mindful of the racism that her unsuspecting adolescent may experience and not fully understand. We must help our children to understand these uncontrollable forces, while at the same time keeping our personal stress levels under control. Further, we must help them to build a strong sense of self-esteem, pride, self-image, self-worth, and, most important, self-love. This can be accomplished with activities that will help children feel good about themselves. And we must show our children where they can shine, and when they do, we must *be there* to give them praise. Because African American mothers must be the stress buffers for their children, they must learn stress-proofing strategies themselves that can help temper the encounters with racism their children will confront. By placing stress buffers in their paths, we may be able to reduce the number of stressful encounters we have with them as well.

CHAPTER 4

Stressors at Work

GENDER AND RACE ISSUES IN BLACK AND WHITE

As the social and economic climate in America continues to deteriorate, particularly since September 11, and as more jobs are lost to Third World countries and to a rapidly growing global economy in which China, for example, floods U.S. markets with limited reciprocal agreements, I am reminded of what my grandmother used to say: "I'm just trying to hold onto this old piece of job." During the 1930s and 1940s, my grandmother was often threatened by job losses due to an oppressive, nonprotective work environment and from white women who entered the job market to make up for the loss of white male employees who were fighting World War II. African American women were already in low-paying jobs. Many white women replaced African American women by taking the better jobs and relegating African Americans to the more unpleasant ones. In fact, in Detroit in 1942, the "Ford Motor Company had openly refused to hire blacks in general and black women in particular" (Scott 1991, p. 28). It was not until the NAACP and the 1963 march on Washington that some of these white-only jobs were made available to African American women. However, unskilled African American women "got the most dangerous and grueling jobs" with low pay. They found themselves working in stifling "dope rooms," filled with nauseating glue fumes, while white unskilled women worked in well-ventilated sewing rooms. Black women, exclusively, held jobs in the sintering plants, where the air was filled with ore dust and heated by blast furnaces. Even professional African American women had to bear the brunt of discrimination, like the six professional college-trained Women Army Corps (WACS) nurses who were court-martialed because they refused to accept kitchen duties while their white nursing counterparts held motor pool or medicine-related jobs (Scott 1991, p. 26). Without having a full understanding of the psychosocial aspects of racism in white America, my grandmother must have found this situation and the stress she faced on a daily basis unbearable. My grandmother died from a massive heart attack at the young age of fifty.

As I have noted elsewhere, stress takes its toll on African American women, who are experiencing record numbers of stress-related heart attacks and strokes. As recently reported, stress is number one on the list of daily challenges in a U.S. Department of Labor survey of a quarter-million women (Eberlein 1998). The National Institute for Occupational Safety and Health reports that stress-related disorders are fast becoming the most prevalent reason for worker-disability claims (www.convoke .com/markjr/cjstress.html).

AFRICAN AMERICAN WOMEN WORKING OUTSIDE THE HOME: NOT A CHOICE BUT A MATTER OF SURVIVAL

Historically, African American women have always worked outside the home. In fact, they were brought to America to work, and they did. They worked first as indentured servants, then as slaves. When the first black slaves landed in Virginia in 1619, among them were three females who immediately went to work for white slave owners. By 1790, when the first national census was released, there were 4 million slaves—out of a total Southern population of 12 million—who were working to build America. The number of slaves brought to America continued to grow because the American economy depended on their free labor.

In the 1920s, 58 percent of African American single women and 45 percent of single white women worked outside their homes, while a mere 6.5 percent of married white women and 32.5 percent of black married women worked outside the home (Wilson and Russell 1996, p. 163). As you can see, African American women have always worked in record numbers. For example, in the 1920s, 90.5 percent of African American women worked outside the home as compared to 51.5 percent of white women. Yet white women, in much smaller numbers, moved ahead of their African American counterparts to lighter and better-paying jobs, while the African American women were relegated to the "not so pleasant" jobs. The economy flourished when women were in the paid workforce, yet "poor whites, especially those who were married, felt stigmatized by having to work" (Wilson and Russell 1996, p. 63).

Following World War II, when the troops returned home, white men expected to take back their privileged jobs. Now it was time for women

Table 4.1
White, African, and Hispanic American Women's Occupations

Share of Positions Held	White	Black	Hispanic
Doctor	22.3	4.2	5.2
Nurses	93.8	9.3	2.9
Teachers (colleges & universities)	42.5	5.0	2.9
Teachers other schools	74.9	8.6	4.3
Librarians	84.1	10.5	3.7

Source: Shapiro (1995), p. 37.

(especially privileged white women), to return to their homes, and the tug-of-war on the job front began in America.

In the 1960s, with the passage of the Civil Rights Act of 1964, the Voting Rights Act of 1965, and the Immigration Act of 1965, African American people and white women felt they had gained some legal protection. In 1972, the establishment of the Equal Employment Opportunity Act outlawed discrimination by public employers on the basis of race, color, religion, sex, or national origin. Further, "There is a perception among many Black women that feminists' [particularly white women's] demands to be treated like a minority in the workplace have hurt the Black community. Plum positions that were once designated for African Americans, including many in the corporate sector, are now filled by White women." To some black women, "It seems as though White women are eager to advance their own careers at the expense of women who are Black" (Wilson and Russell 1996, p. 165). As you can see in Table 4.1, African American women's benefits from these laws have been minimal: white women are still employed in better jobs. African American women are predominantly in those occupations (service) that in a slave society would be reserved for slaves (Ezorsky 1995, p. 168).

White women continue to make gains in the workforce, creating a solid base for their families. They have not returned home. In fact, in 1988, the Bureau of the Census reported that 55.3 percent of married white women were in the labor force, while 65.8 percent of black women held jobs (Wilson and Russell 1996, p. 63). And white women in 1989 made an average of $318 a week while their African American counterparts made just $238 a week. When African American women encounter these inequities in the workplace, it can become very stressful.

Table 4.2
Occupation and Employment, 1960–1990, White and Black Women

	White		Black	
	1960	1990	1960	1990
White collar	58.1	72.5	18.2	57.7
Blue collar	18.4	9.9	15.2	14.5
Services	23.5	17.6	66.6	27.8

Source: Adapted from Hacker (1992), p. 233.

Was there much change in the job market for African American women in the 1990s at the professional levels? Are African American women taking jobs from their white (male and female) colleagues and counterparts? Table 4.2 answers that question. And the answer is no.

Who has benefited from the set-aside programs such as Affirmative Action, Civil Rights, and Equal Employment Opportunity? As Wilson and Russell (1996, p. 171) point out, "In 1994 the Illinois Minority Female Business Enterprise Program awarded $140 million to White businesswomen and $21.6 million to Black businesswomen." So I ask you again: who benefited? I am sure the sisters in Illinois must have experienced some stress, knowing that their black relatives were the ones who had been beaten, castrated, and hanged, prompting the Civil Rights Act, yet they still lagged behind white women in gaining the benefits from that act. This and other similar problems discussed later, and the results presented by the *Working Women* Magazine survey, may have contributed to the rift that emerged between some African American and white women.

Greene and Greene reports in *Working Women* Magazine's salary update issue (Greene and Greene 1995) on the best-paid women in corporate America. Based on that published list, it appeared that none of these women were minorities. All twenty women earned enormous salaries; in particular, Linda Wachner's salary rose 27 percent to $2.36 million (p. 36). Here are just a few of these female CEO's and president's salaries:

President	Tootsie Roll	Ellen Gordon	Salary $545,000	Total comp: $1.3 million
CEO	Mattel Toys	Jill Borad	Salary $628,237	Total comp: $1.79 million
CEO	Fox Broadcasting	Lucie Salhonz	Salary $1.5 million	
CEO	Gap Kids	Patricia DeRose	Salary $518,884	Total comp: $1.06 million
CEO	Ann Taylor	Sally F. Kasaks	Salary $650,000	Total comp: $901,505

In a special report "2000 Catalyst Census of Women Corporate Officers and Top Earners," it was reported that "The percentage of women among America's top executives increased from 8.7% in 1995 to 12.5% in 2000. However, since Catalyst began separately tracking women of color in 1999, their percentage among top executives has not changed from 1.35%. Women of color accounted for 10.3% of the 1,297 women officers at the 400 Fortune 500 companies that participated in the survey (84 African Americans, 27 Asians/Pacific Islanders, 21 Hispanics and 2 others)" (Scott 2001, p. 30).

In another Catalyst survey reported by Scott (2001), "Minority Women Hit a 'Concrete Ceiling,' " there was little change with regard to inequality in the workplace, even when there was a corporate diversity initiative. Catalyst reported that 47 percent of the 1,700 women of color who responded "believe that opportunities for advancement in their companies have improved over the past five years" (p. 30) and 60 percent of white women also noted a positive change. The minority respondents (38 percent African American, 33 percent Hispanic, 27 percent Asian American) cited barriers such as not having an "influential mentor and exclusion from informal networking with colleagues and a lack of exposure to high-visibility assignments [for hampering] their success" (p. 30) (A similar scenario is also playing out in higher education and will be discussed later.) As a result of these problems, "[n]early 73 percent of respondents said they intend to leave their company and one-third of the respondents agree that diversity programs created a positive working environment" (p. 30). Further reported were the efforts of Hallmark Cards in Kansas City, Missouri, to increase minority representation in its senior management. With 7 percent of Hallmark's senior positions held by minorities and 30 percent by women at that time, we can assume that white women hold the vast majority of that 30 percent. At least Hallmark has a plan to increase the proportion of its minority executives.

In another poll, conducted October 10, 2001, *Black Career Women* collected responses from Web site visitors who were asked to respond to the following question: "Has the career advancement of white women had any effect on the career advancement of black women?" Here are the responses:

Positive Effect	11 (24%)
Negative Effect	15 (33%)
No Effect	11 (24%)
Uncertain	8 (17%)

As you can see from these results, some respondents felt that white women have had a negative effect on the career opportunities of black women. How this negative effect has hurt black women was not explained by the survey results.

What's in store for this new century? Will the workplace become more stressful? Or have the upper limits of stress been reached? In 1990, 40 percent of employee turnover was due to stress and 1 million employees per day were absent from work due to stress-related disorders. In 1993 there was an estimated loss of 80 million working days among 17,000 health professionals due to mental problems (Spiegel, Bloom, and Kraemer 1993). Seventy-five to 90 percent of doctor visits are for stress-related illnesses (Childre 1994). No matter where it comes from or who generates the stress in your work environment, the way you perceive it and react to it will have an impact on how long you survive in the workplace.

CONFLICT, STRESS, AND COWORKERS

As you attempt to do your job, those who supervise your work performance can also be a source of stress. White women and men have very different motives for oppressing blacks, particularly African American women. For white men, both racism and sexism may be at work. For white women, racism alone is the culprit. What is important to this discussion is how they act out their racist behaviors in the workplace. Because racist behavior can be a source of stress, the next two sections explore this topic in greater detail. However, when you couple this racist behavior with other stressful interactions with your peers, this can certainly compound the effects of stress. For example, in her article "Coworkers From Hell and How to Cope," Manfred (1996) presents nine employee behavioral types and the stress they generate as well as how to deal with it. When you read the following synopsis, you may recognize some people with whom you are currently working, or you may have a friend whose colleagues at work have some of the following behavioral characteristics. In my career I have encountered all nine of these coworkers (not all at once, thank God).

Manfred starts with the *Petty Bureaucrat.* This is the person who is the gatekeeper. She may report to someone important (say, the CEO) or she may control something everyone needs (like supplies). Then there is the *Credit Grabber.* This may be your boss or a coworker who takes credit for your ideas. Next is one of the most vicious, the *Backstabber.* Ruthless is her middle name. She is the colleague who starts rumors about you. "Rumormongering" is her most common and malignant tactic. Even more insidious, she remains friendly toward you. The *Non-stop Talker* jams you up by running her mouth about office politics. This colleague takes up your valuable time. The *Alarmist* is the carrier of the doomsday story. She's always there to cast any changes (downsizing, for instance) in the most horrific terms. Completely relentless is the *Control Freak.* Overwhelmed with her own job, she puts roadblocks in your way to control your actions. It is hard to find an employment situation today without at least one

Snoop. She reads upside down, reads everything on your desk, or she reads material left mistakenly at the copier. She usually does not use what she has found out against you, but she gossips. As Manfred states, you want to say to the *Snoop,* "Get a life." The *Put-Down Artist* is the one who rubs you wrong every chance she gets. Finally, there's the *Bully.* Her tactics include threatening you during your yearly evaluation or putting your ideas down, only to restate them later as her own (Manfred 1996, pp. 147–148). I have added two other employee types—the Racist and the Sexist. The *Racist* believes that she is privileged and this entitles her to every job, regardless of her qualifications, while the *Sexist* is usually a male who can't keep his eyes off your breasts, his hands off your butt, and his comments to himself. How I suggest you handle some of these employees will be discussed later.

In the workplace, African American females may experience harassment from both white and black males and females. How African American women react to individuals with these characteristics can add to their level of stress or be deadly if allowed to continue.

African American Women versus White American Women in the Workplace

Women who are employed spend the majority of their day at work. When you look at your twenty-four-hour day, you work eight hours, with an hour's travel time, equaling nine hours, and, if you are lucky, you sleep eight hours, for a total of seventeen hours. This leaves you with a mere seven hours for children, dinner, laundry, shopping, and husband. No wonder we're stressed out.

Adding to that stress is the poor working relationship that some African American women and white women are experiencing. By no means are *all* white and black women fighting on the job; however, from the data presented previously, there are problems. If you are one of the African American women experiencing some of these difficulties, this chapter may help you identify what is behind this poor relationship, or it may give you some insight into why your sister, mother, aunt, or cousin complains about work. More importantly, some African American women may bring the stress of a tension-filled workday home, and this needs to be confronted and controlled.

Historical Perspective on the Relationship between Black and White Women

To better understand this mounting rift and struggle in the workplace between black and white women, let's take a historical look at the development of their relationship. This may help to shed some light on why they interact the way they do in the workplace.

African American women, as mentioned previously, have always worked; it was never a sin, and work was expected. White women's morality in colonial America was governed by a strict value code that her white husband adhered to and held her accountable for. This meant that white women were placed on a pedestal—a trophy to show off, not someone to work outside the home. As Wilson and Russell (1996, p. 114) state, "White women were expected to feign a total lack of interest in matters of the flesh, except as a means to have children [and they] were never free to be seductive or act passionate with the men they loved." This may have been one of the reasons why white slave masters sexually preyed upon innocent African slave women.

On the other hand, during the colonial era not only were black women expected to work from sunup to sundown, they were also expected to be obedient bed partners to their white slave masters. Therefore, white women turned their grief outward, lashing out at slave women who they knew made a difference in their white husband's love life. Yes, she knew he was bedding his favorite slave. In fact, there are numerous recorded situations (Sterling 1984, p. 26) where white males would disrespect their wives outright. In one record of divorce cases, it is cited that white men used slave women as pawns in an unpleasant game with their wives. In numerous petitions for divorce, the wife charged that her husband had brought his slave to "his own wife's bed and there carried out his licentious designs; in some instances these were carried out in her presence" (Sterling 1984, p. 26). These slave-master encounters yielded many mulatto or "yaller" children. These children born to the white master were a constant reminder to his wife of the master's infidelity. White women, in order to save face, attempted to look the other way. Rather than coming to the defense of the unprotected female slave, it would infuriate the mistress as the slave's children grew up and started looking like the white master. At the first opportunity, she would sell the children off one by one. Regardless of how brutal the slave master was to his female slaves, even white women did not protest. During pregnancy, if a female slave refused to engage in sex, the master would sometimes force her to dig a hole in the ground and put her pregnant stomach in the hole while the master beat her, and would then sell her child (Sterling 1984, p. 39). For many African American women, the selling of slave children was a heart-wrenching event, and some could not handle it. As reported in New Orleans, a master "owned a woman who was the mother of several children. And when her babies would get about a year or two of age, he'd sell them and it would break her heart. She never got to keep them. When her fourth baby was about two months old, she just studied all the time about how she would have to give it up, and one day she said, 'I'm not going to let old master sell this baby, he just ain't going to do it.' She got up and gave it something out of a bottle and pretty soon it was dead" (Sterling 1984, p. 58).

African American female slaves were tormented because of their sexuality: white men lusted over them and white women loathed them for it.

White and Black Women in the Twenty-first Century Workplace

This friction that occurred early on in the development of white and black women's relationships in the United States made a lasting, embedded impact that may rear its ugly head at any given point in these women's lives, making their working relationship difficult, if not totally impossible. Some white women are raised from birth with the notion that their white, privileged status makes them superior to others. When these attitudes are brought into the workplace, it can become unbearable not only for the women who are the direct targets of this attitude but also for other employees (for example, a secretary who is asked to type scathing memos to an African American female employee). Also, many of the white women who live with white males and work in corporate America begin to emulate the behavior of the white males with whom they are in closest contact. Further, the management style of a white woman is often modeled after the strongest and most influential person in her life—her white father, uncle, brother, or husband. Yet, white women are socialized by white males (their fathers) to behave in a subordinate and obedient manner. African American females are also socialized by their fathers, but their socialization is not grounded in privilege. In the workplace, white females tend to side with white males and closely mirror their behavior toward black women, which is grounded in oppression, exploitation, and subordination. To illustrate this position, the writing of Paulo Freire is offered.

In *Pedagogy of the Oppressed* (1968), Paulo Freire explored the relationship between the oppressor and the oppressed. In this analysis, he posits that "Because of their identification with the oppressor [for the purposes of this discussion, white men], they [for this discussion, white women] have no consciousness of themselves as persons or as members of an oppressed class . . . the oppressed find in the oppressor their model of manhood" (Freire 1968, pp. 30–31). In other words, the close identification that white women have with white men as their oppressors, leads them to become just like them—oppressors of others. These white women then oppress all those with whom they come in contact, turning the oppressed into the oppressor. Oppressors do not view their privilege as a means of taking from others. In fact, according to Freire (1968, p. 45), the oppressor believes it's an inalienable right to have more and if the others do not have it, it's their fault "because they are incompetent and lazy . . . [and] the oppressed are regarded as potential enemies who must be watched." This, in part, may account for the oversupervision of African American women in the workplace and the overpolicing of the black community.

Often, white women function as pawns for white males because of how they have been oppressed and socialized. Oppressive behavior by white women, coupled with unearned privileges (in part due simply to having white skin), can be deadly in a workplace environment. To illustrate how white women are given the opportunity to exercise this privilege even when they unknowingly (however, I doubt it) take advantage of the unearned privilege, I offer Peggy McIntosh's (1992, p. 71) interpretation.

In her article "White Privilege and Male Privilege," McIntosh identified "forty-six ordinary and daily ways in which [white women] experience having white privilege, by contrast with [their] African American colleagues" (p. 71). I have selected a sample of these experiences, situations that, when encountered by African American women, become sources of stress because African American women cannot make these affirmative statements that white women take for granted.

1. White women can go shopping alone most of the time, fairly well assured that she will not be followed or harassed by a store detective.

2. White women can turn on the television or open to the front page of the paper and see people of her race widely and positively represented.

3. When white women are told about their national heritage or about "civilization," they are shown that people of their color made it what it is.

4. White women can be sure that their children will be given curricular materials that testify to the existence of their race.

5. White women can be pretty sure of finding a publisher for this piece on white privilege.

6. When white women use checks, credit card, or cash, they can count on their skin color not to work against the appearance that they are financially reliable.

7. White women do not have to educate their children to be aware of systemic racism for their own daily physical protection.

8. White women can be pretty sure that their children's teachers and employers will tolerate them if they fit school and workplace norms; their chief worries about their children do not concern others' attitude toward their race.

9. White women are never asked to speak for all the people of their racial group.

10. If a traffic cop pulls a white woman over or if the IRS audits her tax return, she can be sure she hasn't been singled out because of her race.

11. White women can be pretty sure that an argument with an African American colleague is less likely to jeopardize her chances for advancement than to jeopardize theirs.

12. White women can be fairly sure that if they argue for the promotion of a person of another race, or a program centering on race, this is not likely to cost

them heavily within their present setting, even if their colleagues disagree with them.

13. White women can worry about racism without being seen as self-interested or self-seeking.

14. A white woman can take a job with an affirmative action employer without having her co-worker on the job suspect that she got it because of her race.

15. White women can be pretty sure of finding people who would be willing to talk with them and advise them about their next step professionally.

16. A white woman can be sure that if she needs legal or medical help, her race will not work against her.

17. White women can easily find academic courses and institutions that give attention to only people of their race.

The McIntosh taxonomy of privileges recognizes that "some privileges make me [a White woman] feel at home in the world. Others allow me [white women] to escape penalties or dangers that others suffer" (McIntosh 1992, p. 76). This suffering is what white women infuse into the workplace, making it a stressful environment. Unfortunately, many of these white women colleagues and managers do not understand their own behavior, which, in turn, makes African American women suffer from stress-related illnesses. That is why it is so important for their longevity that it is included in this discussion.

Despite the popular belief that affirmative action policies give unfair advantages to blacks in general, as of 1991 only 7.2 percent of black women (and black men) were executives, administrators, or managers in corporate America. This figure compares to 12 percent of white women in similar jobs and 14.7 percent of white men. African American women, no matter how well they are prepared, still face the notion that they are benefiting from unearned privileges lavished by affirmative action programs. For example, Julianne Malveaux (1997), in her article "The Myth of Educational Attainment: When a Black Woman's Master's Degree Equals a White Woman's Bachelor's Degree," reports on the controversial lawsuit—*Taxman v. Piscataway Board of Education*. In this case, the Piscataway, New Jersey, Board of Education cut several teaching positions. Two teachers whose jobs were initially cut—one white and one black—"were hired the same day and deemed 'equally' qualified, and the school board justified retaining Williams [the black teacher] on the basis of diversity" (Malveaux 1997, p. 33). Taxman (the white teacher) filed a lawsuit that was settled out of court because, rather than claiming it was retaining the black teacher because of her qualifications, including her master's degree, the board chose to retain her because she increased the diversity of the teaching staff. As a result of the board's bad decision, Taxman "put her life on hold, apparently because she could not stand the notion that some black woman should get a job she thought she should have. Never mind that the black woman, her colleague, had more education. Never mind that her colleague was a better teacher. Taxman is white and she has wrapped herself in the privilege of Whiteness. Thus, her lawsuit" (Malveaux 1997, p. 33). Knowing that she was qualified for the position, the stress that the black teacher (Williams) must have gone through had to be unbearable.

There are, however, workplace strategies that have been implemented to reduce blood pressure among African American women in the workplace. I mentioned one such intervention strategy here and several in part II. Webb, Smyth, and Yarandi (2000) taught a seven-muscle group progressive relaxation intervention in the workplace to reduce blood pressure. These African American women used various relaxation techniques and, consequently, there was a difference in the systolic (top number) blood pressure. This study supports the use of the workplace to help African American women with personal strain that they may encounter (Webb, Smyth, and Yarandi 2000). Every day in the work world, African American women struggle to keep themselves employed. And some of this struggle and stress emanates from some white women's treatment of them. The following examples illustrate how some white women create a stressful work environment for their African American colleagues:

CASE I: STRESS IN THE HIGHER EDUCATION WORK ENVIRONMENT

A college professor, Dr. Flood (not her real name), with excellent credentials, including a teaching certificate, a doctorate, and extensive teaching experience and publications, knew that her workplace would be difficult when, her first week on the job, a white male colleague warned, and I quote, "Don't do too much scholarly work here." She pushed the incident to the back of her mind and continued working with her students, writing, publishing, speaking, doing committee work, and team-teaching with a senior white female colleague who had taken Dr. Flood under her wing. With her colleague's support, obtaining tenure was a breeze. When her next book was published and her popularity increased among her students, community leaders, and other colleagues, she remained satisfied with her position. Things were relatively quiet, except for some demands made by the dean that were not Dr. Flood's responsibility. One of Freire's (1968) theories is that the oppressor must keep the oppressed from uniting with allies and, therefore, must keep the oppressed distracted and confused. Within a few weeks of hearing of the dean's demands, Dr. Flood received a phone call from a black student who informed her that one of Dr. Flood's white female colleagues had come to the student with a proposition. The conversation had gone like this: "Colleagues can't go after another colleague—it would not look good—so I want you [the student] to ask some of the other students in Dr. Flood's class if they were having problems getting in touch with her. And if they say yes, I want you to get them to write a letter of complaint to her Dean." What the complaining/backstabbing white female professor did not know was that a similar incident had happened to this black student in her workplace, where she had had no warning. She vowed to never let it happen to anyone else. So she warned Dr. Flood. The student was called several times and harassed about securing the information from her classmates. She spoke to other students, who reported having no problem reaching Dr. Flood. When the student reported back to the white female backstabber, she was not pleased. The black female student then began to experience difficulty with this faculty member. In the last conversation that Dr. Flood had with this student, the student was considering leaving the university. Remember, not everyone is given a warning.

Some black women buy into and are also used as pawns against their black sisters (this will be discussed later) for a variety of reasons—to earn a degree, to secure a contract renewal, to get tenure, or just to be the "Head Nigger in Charge" (HNIC). These kinds of workplace situations can be stressful. Dr. Flood made sure that from that day on she documented all incidents with this faculty member and sought the advice of an attorney.

One of Dr. Flood's strategies was to make sure that her accomplishments were always noted by the administration (keeping up her credibility before the university community), and she documented in a journal every encounter with this white female colleague/backstabber who has since backed off. Why was this white female colleague attacking a black female colleague? Or was it just sheer mean-spiritedness (the *Backstabber*)? There is "some evidence that some whites in desegregated workplaces resent a black employee daring to do the same job as a white or to do better in performing that job" (Feagin and Sikes 1995, p. 149).

Another of my African American female colleagues reported the following situation in her dealings with a white female supervisor and her subordinates:

Even though I am a product of the education system of a White state institution, I was not part of any quota system; I paid for my education the "American" way: through student loans. However, because I aspired to the highest level, i.e. a Ph.D., I became conspicuously visible to that same institution as a means to their end. The undergraduate component of that conglomerate decided to try to increase their quotas by offering me a part-time position on the way to a full-time "minority line" already in the making. The interim part-time position was being held by a white female, who then moved up to a full-time assistant to the boss position. The minority line became available and I was keyed.

[This position] fit white society's idea of a minority line—director of a program as part of an articulation agreement between two diametrically opposed institutions, both wanting the same body of students (minorities), and dual appointment as faculty and administrator. Even though the other institution was a junior [college], they were traditional (the [first institution] was not), so both institutions had conflicting agendas. I was in the middle—not expecting to win. There was nothing to win. White institutions do not want a lot of black students, or black faculty. From the beginning, the white "assistant to the boss" was troubled because she wanted the special minority classification to apply to her also when it was convenient, but not to undermine her inherent privilege. She became my nemesis in the ensuing years, so much so [that] when she was elevated to "boss," I was her first target in asserting power. The mantra used was "Where are the minority students you are to raise?" The plan to give me permanent appointment, not tenure, worked, until it was time for me to graze in more creative pastures in a black institution and the white female boss was affirmed. Research has shown that Affirmative Action has benefited that group more than any other.

    The other statement—"To blame this faculty when it was evident that the institution had no commitment to this particular population"—is another example of how institutional insidious racism manifests itself and seeks to erode the psychic fabric of its target, even though it may be unsuccessful.

This faculty member has since relocated to another institution where she is a contributing member of the college community, where she is welcomed, and where her scholarly ability is treasured and appreciated.

    Although "many colleges and universities have responded to some degree to pressure from the black community to hire more black faculty members . . . black faculty members who are hired in white colleges often find themselves to be among a small number of black representatives in a mostly white world, sometimes with little chance of long term survival there" (Feagin and Sikes 1995, p. 160). Often in these universities and colleges, white female deans and/or chairs spend most of their time overly supervising black faculty. The apparent need to follow this faculty employee stems from the notion of questioning the worker's ability to perform in the faculty role. Some white females have been indoctrinated with the stereotype of shiftless, no-account blacks who bear watching to see if they do the job. Some white coworkers benefit from this shift of attention away from them, allowing them to do whatever they choose because the white supervisor is busy watching someone else. In fact, some white faculty will complain about a black faculty in order to shift attention away from them, to keep the white female supervisor's focus on the black faculty.

    One faculty member handled this kind of situation by making sure that her actions when dealing with students were always documented (for example, all phone calls and meetings to explain the reasons for poor grades). If faced with a lawsuit, a daily diary provides needed evidence; it also serves as a coping tool because it is cathartic to excrete from your psyche the experiences you have encountered. Thus, the stress is somewhat abated. Also, isolating oneself, changing work hours, and wearing a big smile when in the company of other faculty and supervisors always keeps your stress level under control.

Institutions of higher education by no means have a monopoly on the unfair treatment of African American female employees, as you can see from the next example.

CASE II: DEFENDING AGAINST THE UNEQUAL TREATMENT OF BLACKS

Another African American woman interviewed for this book, Ms. Vergie (not her real name), reported that she worked in a three-woman office in a small Pennsylvania city. Observing how poorly African American clients were treated when they requested services (spoken to in an unprofessional manner, for example), she spoke out. This resulted in her transfer to another three-woman office where she was again supervised by another white female. The poor treatment of black customers continued at that new location and once again she complained. Ms. Vergie was asked to stay late one evening, allegedly because her supervisor's supervisor (a white male) would be in that evening to offer in-service company training. When the other three employees left for the day, the supervisor fired her, she was told to leave, and she did. When I interviewed Ms. Vergie, I asked her why she had been fired. Her response was "I don't know. They did not tell me." I also asked if she was given anything in writing, and she said no. Ms. Vergie did not return to work the following day and is now attempting to qualify for unemployment benefits.

The ambush tactics used by some employers must be taken into account when African American women are outspoken in support of their own people. Ms. Vergie's case was a clear setup with no witness or warning. White female supervisors can create a work environment that is extremely unpleasant. As mentioned previously, they will sometimes draw others, including black women, into their plots to help legitimize their attacks.

White racism in the workplace is used to control and impede the progress of African American women in the workplace, as well as to limit the number of African Americans who are seeking employment. How institutional racism plays out in the workplace has been the subject of many books, articles, and other printed and visual reports. Therefore, I will only include excerpts to illustrate how racism is incorporated into management styles and how it is carried out in some work settings.

Many workplaces have become more culturally diverse as a result of the hiring of minority women from various racial and cultural backgrounds. Forced to address this influx of the "new minority female" and to avoid lawsuits, the workplace has turned to cultural diversity training. This is all well and good, if the audience is willing to recognize the need, incorporate strategies to make the workplace more equitable, and apply fair treatment to all who are employed. Problems arise when the employer or employee does not recognize racist behavior directed toward others or when the employer or employee is a closet racist.

The white female employer or supervisor who has been raised in a predominantly white environment, in which African American women are housekeepers, babysitters, and laundry and kitchen personnel, may have a set opinion as to how she will relate to a professional African American woman. How well she interacts with African American women employees will determine how well the work of the organization is accomplished. If she uses racist techniques that are embedded in her psyche as a result of her upbringing, the organization will suffer. Some supervisors do not always recognize racism in their behavior because it is part of their character and personal behavior. For example, a white woman supervisor may attempt to keep a closer eye on her African American female employee and not the other employees simply because she believes that "Blacks are lazy," "Blacks are never on time," and so on. On the other hand, the closet racist will try to be friends with the African American employees, only to turn on them by utilizing information she has gathered through the friendship. In their book *Impacts of Racism on White Americans*, Bowser and Hunt (1996, p. 208) write, "Early Irish immigrants were discriminated against, partly via the label 'white nigger.' Then, when the Irish began to create alliances with blacks in the free labor debates and movement, they were relabeled as white and encouraged to join with other [immigrant] white laborers to resist the advance of free black labor." Racism that depicts whites as inherently superior to people of color solely because of their race has corrupted and hampered the American dream for many.

White females in the workplace are here to stay, regardless of all the efforts from their husbands and the stay-at-home-moms movement, so African American women must learn to deal with them before they adversely affect our physical health. Next we examine a case drawn from the literature that deals with an office environment and the expectations whites have about how African American women should make them feel, and how whites lash out and create a stressful workplace in response.

CASE III: EXPECTATIONS OF WHITES AND THE STRUGGLE TO DO A JOB

In Angela Mitchell and Kennise Herring's book, *What the Blues Is All About* (1997), the authors present the encounter of a sister named Elaine. Elaine tells about coworkers who expected mammy behavior from her, and let her know they were disappointed when she didn't deliver. "I received a less-than-positive [performance] review from my supervisor, which I didn't understand. I knew I had done my job well. When I went in to question the review, my supervisor, a white woman, told me that several of my coworkers [had] complained that I was intimidating and hard to get along with. I knew what she meant—I didn't make them feel good, I didn't make them laugh, put them at ease, socialize with them at lunch. I was there to do a job, but I was being rated on how comfortable I made whites I worked with feel" (Mitchell and Herring 1998, p. 55). Rather than fight back, Elaine retired.

Instead of retiring or being forced out of earning a paycheck, there are other options available, and some will be discussed in later chapters. In the next case, an African American woman in a nonprofit corporation is subjected to an organizational structure that harms those who do not understand how it works—a case of institutional racism.

CASE IV: ANOTHER BLACK WOMAN FIRED FOR CAUSE

Discrimination in the workplace, on the basis of race and sex, is a common phenomenon. Throughout this country, in varied work settings, black, Hispanic, and other minority women are finding themselves victims of increasingly hostile acts, which are rooted in institutional racism. African American women, as mentioned previously, are especially vulnerable to the demonic twins racism and sexism. In fact, the issues resulting from the imposition of racist- and sexist-based tactics and behaviors are sometimes indistinguishable.

Examples of institutional racism and its impact on the careers of black women are pervasive and widespread. It affects us whether we work in factories, in hospitals, in the home, in the corporate world, in the academic world, or in the nonprofit world. Career advances that black women have achieved over the last thirty years have been systematically eroded, especially at the higher levels, and desirable jobs have become scarce. Black women have had to persevere. They still find themselves competing with less educated, less competent white women and must be essentially overqualified for some positions. What African American executives have had to experience is offered here in one female black executive's voice.

In 1993, I was hired as the CEO of a nonprofit, local office of a national organization. In the 60-year history of this organization, I was the first African American CEO. Nationally, I joined the ranks of 160 other CEOs. Of this number only five, including myself, were African American females. Another three CEOs were Hispanic, for a total of eight CEOs of color.

I was no stranger to this organization, both at the local level and at the national level. For over seven years prior to my selection as the CEO, I had volunteered continually with the organization in a variety of roles. I had served on my local affiliate's board of directors as a member and officer. I had served on numerous fund-raising and task force ad hoc committees. In an odd twist of fate, I had been a member of the Search Committee for the new CEO in 1993. I decided to become a candidate for the position only after members of the committee continually urged me to apply for the job, and I saw other candidates who weren't as qualified interview for the job.

I had been very active in regional and national committees and task forces. I served on or chaired numerous committees. I also served as a National Board of Directors member from 1991–1993. My selection as a CEO resulted in my resignation as a Board member. However, I still maintained active involvement on the same committees, only now I represented the CEO constituency.

From my earliest involvement in the organization, one of the issues that I worked tirelessly on was that of cultural diversity within the national organization and local organization. The issue of increasing the number of volunteers and staff from culturally diverse ethnic groups was one that the organization purports to endorse and strives to achieve. Yet this issue is one of the most hotly debated, emotional issues, which the organization continues to address and makes little progress. In spite of a significant move, in which I played an instrumental role, the organization has difficulty making the changes necessary to ultimately achieve a diverse organization. Another problem is that the organization refuses to confront institutional racism within its own ranks.

The organization prospered under my management. I successfully completed three fiscal years with surpluses, which added over a quarter-million dollars to the agency's reserves; increased the level of fund-raising and grants awarded to the organization; improved the agency's visibility and positive acceptance in the African American and Latino communities and in the educational community; rehabbed and expanded the busiest and most productive clinic site; and re-organized the agency for participation in the managed care arena.

After the initial year, these accomplishments and milestones received scant acknowledgment from the Board of Directors. Although I was rated on my performance evaluations consistently as meeting or exceeding expectations, I was also criticized for not "communicating" enough with the Board. In spite of the fact that I wrote numerous progress reports, updates, a newsletter, and gave oral reports at all subcommittee and Board meetings, this criticism continued. Other criticisms followed. I didn't use the Board members' "expertise." And when we entered merger discussions with another organization, I was criticized as not being "enthusiastic" about merger.

My abilities and expertise were questioned, although I found that, initially, the questions were not made face to face. Other Board members who were supportive would tell me about the remarks and attacks that were being made. Increasingly, the Board's President, Vice-President and Treasurer, all women, pressured me to justify my actions and to include them in decisions about the day-to-day operations of the organization. My resistance of these micromanagement tactics served to intensify their efforts to portray me as incompetent and not responsive to the Board. These women were relentless in their determination to control me or get rid of me. As the officers, they ultimately controlled the information disseminated to the other Board members. They conspired to distort, twist into half-truths, and ultimately outright lie about the condition of the agency under my leadership. It would seem odd, except that this is the result of institutional racism, but other Board members chose to ignore the evidence of my good work and to listen to the allegations of my detractors.

In a series of events that are extremely painful to recount, and very convoluted to describe, I fought hard to change the minds of the Board members, keep my job, and maintain my dignity. The harder I fought, however, the more entrenched the "group" became. The supportive Board members, many of them also African Americans, found their voices ignored, dismissed, or discounted. When I finally made the decision to leave the agency, I requested a meeting with the Board and asked for a mutual agreement to sever my contract. In fact, I asked for this at two meetings. I was ignored and patronized by these same Board members who wanted to get rid of me. Unable to resolve the issue in a professional manner, I decided that it was time to engage an attorney.

Apparently, my audacity in seeking legal representation enraged the Board members. It's ironic that those most angered by my actions were the white, female lawyers on the board. At a Board meeting to which I was not invited, a vote was taken to fire me. The next morning when I arrived at my office, I was met, actually I feel to this day that I was ambushed, by four Board members and the agency's attorney. They refused to allow me to enter my office, took me to a restaurant, and told me I was fired. Turn in your keys, and get out! Although I was supposedly fired for cause, they refused to answer my question about the nature of the cause. In another blatant disregard for ethical behavior, one of the Board members, who voted for my firing, resigned from the Board and was appointed to [the position of] CEO. If the reader hasn't guessed by now, I'll tell you that this is another white female.

I believe that the reason that I was fired in the manner I described above was to humiliate and silence me. I was placed in a position to be fired in a public place and by a group of five people! I was not given the opportunity to leave the job with dignity, with the usual fanfare by staff and others, which accompanies such exits (even when it's under duress), because there was the intent by the white women on the Board to humble and disgrace me. I have refused to go quietly, however. I have refused to be silent. I have refused to put a euphemistic label on a brutal, racist, sexist act. My story and others in this book are and should be vivid reminders that institutional racism continues to plague black women, and there is a need to talk about it!

I agree that we must create a venue for the needed conversations.

The situations described in these four cases are by no means representative of all white females. These are but a sampling of some whose attitudes adversely affect their black counterparts. In my effort to educate African American women about their stressors, all women, not only African American women, must understand the problems we are facing and be open to discussing these stressors and bringing them to the Womanist conference table. And we must harness support from one another, when needed, in all workplaces. If this issue is not taken seriously, and if we allow others to shape the role of women in the workplace, all women in the workplace will become "as scarce as hen's teeth."

Recognizing the problems that African American women and white women are experiencing in the workplace, *Essence* magazine and *Ladies Home Journal* held a roundtable discussion regarding workplace issues. As Audrey Edwards reports in her article "Black and White: What Still Divides Us?"(1998, p. 138), "Before both sides can talk, they have to become comfortable with the racial and cultural differences each bring to the table and recognize that different doesn't have to mean divided." And once we all come to the realization that we probably have similar wants, how we get them will be up to us.

African American Women versus African American Women in the Workplace

African American women in the workplace are placed under an enormous amount of stress because of their gender and their race—a double whammy. Faced with fighting two prejudices, you would naturally think that this would unite them in a common bond to fight these workplace forces. Instead, African American women in the workplace create a different set of stressors for each other. Some of these stressors are the residual effects of slave behaviors and other manipulative forces within the realm of racism and sexism.

African American women entered the job market first as indentured servants; then as slaves, doing everyone's work; then as domestics, doing all the jobs white women refused to do; and finally as teachers, nurses, and social workers, doing jobs that did not take them out of their nurturing role or the "other mother" role. In the twentieth century, they bucked the corporate world and demanded a professional role once held by white males, as they prepared to take on the glass ceiling, or the concrete ceiling, that prevented them from developing skills for the twenty-first century. After great sacrifices, they managed to accomplish some of their workplace goals but were met with resistance from some of their African American sisters. Clawing their way into the better jobs, fighting with white women, white women's husbands, and sometimes their own black brothers (discussed in the next section), they now faced their own black sisters. Some, but not all, lost their real sisterhood and became pawns for those who would rather see them in the kitchen than in the boardroom. As the African American woman struggled to keep her job, other forces required her to behave in certain ways, deemed "black." This had one purpose: to divide and conquer, as described in the next section.

Historical Perspective on the Relationship between Black Women

To better understand why this constituted a purposeful plot, consider two pieces of relevant literature: "Let's Make a Slave" (1970) and *Pedagogy of the Oppressed* (Freire 1968). In Fredrick Douglas's preamble to "Let's Make a Slave," he states, "They [whites] watched . . . with skilled and practiced eyes, and learned to read, with great accuracy, the state of mind and heart of slaves" (p. 2). In other words, they sized up African American people and then developed a plan to oppress them, using various tactics, including some involving African American people themselves. One twenty-first-century residual effect may be black-on-black crime. As noted in "Let's Make a Slave," the plan that was developed "describes the rationale and results of the Anglo-Saxon's ideas and methods of insuring the master/slave relationship" (p. 1). Described are the ingredients, that is, nigger man, nigger women, and nigger baby. The analogy used was to the breaking of a horse. The overriding principle was to take away their natural state and make them dependent on the white man. How white society sustained that dependency was very important and necessary to preventing any economic problems. The following are "the necessary principles for long range comprehensible economic planning" (p. 2):

a) Both horses and nigger are no good to the economy in the wild or natural state.
b) Both must be broken and tied together for orderly production.
c) For orderly futures, special and particular attention must be paid to the female and the youngest offspring.
d) Both must be crossbred to produce a variety and division of labor.
e) Both must be taught to respond to a peculiar new language.
f) Psychological and physical instruction of containment must be created for both.

The oppression scenario continues and, for this analysis, the breaking of the female slave is very relevant because it has all the elements of what we see in some of African American women's behavior today. First, in keeping with the plan, in the presence of the female you break the male by burning him, beating him, and tying him to horses, splitting him apart. You are thus removing the female's protection, making the male weak in her mind, and planting fear in her heart-frozen psychological state. In this state of mind, the fear she has for her young male son will make her reverse the roles of her children, making the male dependent on her and the female independent—a role reversal. Once in place, you will have, according to this theory, created a submissive dependent male in the midst of an orbiting cycle that turns on its axis forever. African American mothers fear the treatment of their male children, from the threat of castration, to an incarceration rate 250 percent higher than that for white males, racial profiling, and driving while black (DWB). All these serve to increase African American women's stress levels. Faced with stress every time her son leaves home, African American mothers have been manipulated and molded into the plot. And, according to this scenario, the result is "You've got the nigger women out front and the nigger man behind and scared" ("Let's Make a Slave" 1970, p. 3).

In the workplace, women bring with them their experiences, some of them pleasant, others unpleasant. How they handle interactions with other women may reflect remnants of this plot and role reversal.

On a daily basis, some African American women are faced with other African American women who are not supportive of their efforts in the workplace. For an African American woman in this position, this will certainly increase her stress level and how she feels about her black sisters. Rooted in the history of slavery is another white American–crafted plot—using the housebroken slave (light-skinned complexion, white master's offspring) against the field slave (darker-skinned) to foster jealousy, distrust, and envy in the hearts and minds of slaves. These light-complexioned slaves supposedly were treated better, if you count being raped at eleven years old and used sexually by any white male who visited the plantation better treatment. This strategy of dividing African Americans has continued for centuries throughout America, with employers, including movie producers, hiring and promoting the lighter skinned blacks from the magnificent spectrum of African American skin colors. This further exacerbates the divisiveness crafted by mean-spirited white Americans.

Other aspects of the slave era are carried over into the workplace as well. Black women are expected to look and behave in certain ways that make whites feel comfortable with their presence. For example, consider the following stereotypical roles: *nurturer*, caretaker of white people's children; *sapphire*, the happy-go-lucky, to whom whites can confide anything and the African American woman is supposed to smile; *mammy*, someone to help them when they need a listening ear that is nonjudgmental. If African American women step out of these stereotypical roles in the workplace, they are slapped with a derogatory label (such as too aggressive or militant). How much of this leftover behavioral molding and role expectation affects African American women in their relationships in the workplace is best demonstrated in the following cases.

As Dr. French (not her real name) reported, she had not experienced a deliberate attack by another African American woman until a junior faculty member complained to their white female supervisor.

CASE V: A BACKSTABBER II—THE HNIC SYNDROME

Dr. French, a senior-level faculty member, had a relationship with her white female supervisor that required constant vigilance. This supervisor had successfully forced another African American woman to leave the job and was known in the community as a woman who had gotten rid of her African American female administrative assistant before coming to the university. When the junior faculty was hired, she was aware of the supervisor's reputation with regard to other black women who worked for the university. When a student misunderstood some information about an academic process that Dr. French had told him to convey to the black female junior faculty, the junior faculty member chose not to request clarification from Dr. French but rather to complain to the white female supervisor. Dr. French, after receiving a negative written memo from the supervisor, went to the female junior faculty and explained the situation to her. She appeared to accept Dr. French's explanation and the matter was dropped. However, within a month, another miscommunication occurred between Dr. French and the junior faculty member and once again the junior faculty member went to the supervisor. As a result, the supervisor sent another negative memo to Dr. French. Fortunately, Dr. French was a well-seasoned, tenured faculty member who was aware of the academic personnel process. Therefore, she guarded her personnel file by inserting written rebuttals to all the negative memos or e-mails she received. Most disturbing was the fact that this junior faculty was a talented, competent academician, but she had forgotten where she came from and was being used as a pawn against her own black sister. I offer this one example because there is a paucity of information in the literature regarding the relationship among African American females in the workplace. However, I am sure that this is not the only workplace situation of its kind.

African American Women versus White Men in the Workplace

African American women's historical relationship with white men has been one of exploitation, objectification, and rejection. Because white male power is largely predicated on African American female subordination, few black women entertain delusions of sharing that power and enjoying the privileges attached to white male power. And, as mentioned previously, most white women identify with white males and take on some of their management styles. This translates into clashes with African American women employees.

Table 4.3
Comparing Paychecks: Median Annual Earnings as a Share of White Men's
Earnings

	Black Men	Hispanic Men	White Women	Black Women	Hispanic Women
1995	74.3	72.1	57.5	55.4	49.3
1993	74.0	64.8	70.8	63.7	53.9
1990	73.1	66.3	69.4	62.5	54.3
1985	69.7	68.0	63.0	57.1	52.1
1980	70.7	70.8	58.9	55.7	50.5

Source: Shapiro (1995), p. 35.

Women in general recognize that male control of their economic well-being shapes their entire life. Women made sixty cents for every dollar earned by males in 1979 and seventy-two cents for every dollar earned by males in 1993 (fifteen years later). In 2003 they earn seventy-six cents for every dollar earned by males.

When you further compare the salaries of white males to black females, white males outrank them even more than they do white females. As you can see from Table 4.3, in 1995 black women made 55.4 percent less than comparable white males, and their white female counterparts made 57.5 percent less than the white males with whom they share privileges, but not pay rates.

It was not until the passage of the Civil Rights Act (1964) and the emergence of the white feminist movement, that demands were made by women for an equal share of the jobs that white males held, including fire-fighters, police officers, soccer coaches, athletic directors, and lawyers. In the 1970s, white males began to experience the pressures of job competition. These pressures also challenged the privileges and status of a white male–dominated job market. Coupled with downsizing, mergers, subcontracting, and temporary workers, a declining need for white-collar jobs has also made jobs scarce, and now, with the economic impact of September 11 and the war with Iraq, the job market is getting more strained.

Should white males be concerned about their employment future? According to Barbara Arnivene and the Lawyers Committee for Civil Rights under Law, "If African Americans are taking all of the jobs, why is there double digit unemployment in the African American community?" (Shapiro 1995, p. 32).

Some white male employees may view African American women as a threat, which may result in your experiencing some stressful moments.

However, white males should understand that while white males make up just 39.2 percent of the population, they account for 82.5 percent of those on the Forbes 400 list (those worth at least $265 million), 77 percent of Congress, 92 percent of state governors, 70 percent of tenured college faculty, almost 90 percent of daily newspaper editors, and 77 percent of television news directors (Gates 1993, p. 49). Further, according to the April 30, 1998, edition of *Black Issues in Higher Education,* the American Council on Education (ACE) reported that most of the nearly 2,300 college presidents were white males. In the same report, it indicated that progress for African Americans seeking the presidency of institutions of higher education has been slow, with an increase of 8.1 percent in 1986, 10.4 percent in 1995, a mere 2.3 percent increase ("Progress Slow for Minorities" 1998, p. 8).

With white males dominating the job market, you would assume that African American women, who are few in numbers in relation to both white males and white females, would not experience as much work-related stress. Think again. In her magazine article "Corporate Race War," on the infamous Texas scandal, Diane Weathers (1997) reported that a black woman, Bari Ellen-Roberts, prepared herself for more than twenty years for the corporate world, holding positions such as vice president for banking at Chase Bank, where she helped manage a $4.5 billion pension fund for Texaco. When Texaco came under fire by the Department of Labor to integrate its predominantly white male management, they offered Roberts a job, which she accepted once the job description she herself authored had been approved. She assumed the role of senior financial analyst at a starting salary of $65,000. During her stay in that position, she took notice of how other white males treated her, some of whom assumed that she was an outside auditor, disregarding the nameplate on her outer office door. The humiliation didn't stop there (and I'm sure neither did her stress level). She was asked for her opinion regarding diversity. She was screamed at and accused of being militant, uppity, and a smart-mouthed "colored girl" (Weathers 1997, p. 80).

Roberts saw the handwriting on the wall and began to practice one of my suggested stress busters—*journaling,* or documenting every work-related encounter. Not only did writing down what was happening to her help her develop legal evidence, but it was also a way of de-stressing. For months she suffered through the constant barrage of insults that culminated when her boss left. Although she was next in line for her boss' position, she was passed over for the promotion and it was given to a man (I assume he was a white male, in keeping with Texaco's corporate culture). When she was directed to train him, this was the ultimate insult, and she filed a lawsuit.

More often then not, a lost opportunity passes by so many of us, who like Roberts, clearly have a legitimate lawsuit (Weathers 1997, p. 82). In fact, the number of charges filed with the Equal Employment Opportunity Commission rose from 62,100 in 1990 to 91,200 in 1994 (Tharp 1995, p. 32). In fact, "nearly four decades after the Civil Rights Act of 1964 gave legal equality to minorities, charges of harassment at work based on race or national origin have more than doubled, to nearly 9,000 a year, since 1990 according to the Equal Employment Opportunity Commission" (Bernstein 2001, p. 65). When Roberts's lawsuit was filed, it was during the time when the "black jelly bean" racial slur was making headlines. Remember the taped conversation of Texaco executives who were planning to destroy files that could help the plaintiffs? In this conversation, Texaco's black employees were compared to black jelly beans that always stuck to the bottom of the jar. No one wants them; therefore, they fall to the bottom of the human resource file. Once this tape became public, a court settlement of $176 million was agreed to ($115 million in damages plus pay raises of at least 10 percent for 1,400 black employees). I'm sure their stress levels subsided as a result.

In another similar case, Lisa Cortes, a record executive for Loose Cannon, a division of PolyGram Records, received similar treatment by her white male employer. She was the only black female among eighty white males and one black male division head and was "denied the access and support accorded others on her level . . . not told of important meetings . . . social events . . . and her immediate supervisor failed to respond to a request for a meeting" (Weathers 1997, p. 84). When PolyGram decided to dismantle her division, Cortes was assured that a news release would be sent out announcing that she was leaving in "good standing." When the news release was not issued, Lisa filed a lawsuit. Her attorney sent her home to write down (remember journaling?) everything that had happened to her that was different from her peers' treatment.

You have to protect yourself from employers who may be waiting to pounce on you, as in the cases of Ms. Vergie and the CEO. For instance, Ms. Roberts, who filed the lawsuit against Texaco, wanted to take work home and needed to check out a laptop computer. She followed the standard procedure of filing a requisition form, and then was told not to bother with the form. Her "mother wit," that inner voice, said "Watch your back." She was correct. When she left the building, security guards ambushed her, looking for the computer, which she had wisely left on her desk.

In another case reported by Joe Feagin and Melvin Sikes (1994) in their book *Living with Racism: The Black Middle Class Experience*, the treatment of a college-educated clerk is presented to demonstrate how white males react to African American females. The clerk stated,

In fact for the past twelve years I've faced discrimination on my job because I work with all men. They feel that the job I do is a man's job. They've often told me, "Go

home. You don't belong here. This is not the place for you." (I'm suing the company now because of that.) When I refused to leave, they started to [put
up] . . . racial pictures, drawings, writings on a calendar, and things of that nature
to try to intimidate me into leaving. I refused to quit, but still I'm in the process of
suing the company. . . . I filed with EEOC first, over a year ago. And when nothing
could be settled with them—I asked for no money at that time—they retaliated
against me. They called me incompetent; even though I ran the place alone, and
had to have someone sit in while I went to listen to them call me incompetent. And
I'm still running the place alone now, in fact, I replaced three men. . . . [T]hey
refused to give me an increase in salary, even though my work increased. . . . Yeah,
it's racism, sexism, because . . . I've heard the blacks called "niggers" and "boys"
and "spooks." (Feagin and Sikes 1994, p. 175)

The clerk continued, "It was the nineteenth of January. . . . Somebody
wrote in the square [on the calendar where 'Dr. Martin Luther King's
Birthday' was printed], 'Niggers Day Off'" (p. 176). In this white
male–dominated work environment, this kind of racist behavior caused
increasing stress for this employee, who also found drawings where lips
on the people were so big they looked like turtleneck sweaters.
  A work environment like those I have just discussed must have been
extremely stressful for these sisters. As you will see from the next example, the workplace can also be harmful to your health.

CASE VI: WHITE MALE SUPERVISORS' RESPONSE TO DIVERSITY: STATE GOVERNMENT

  In another case, Ms. South (not her real name), an administrative assistant, the only African American woman who works in a small department
in a large state university in the Northeast, decided to file a discrimination
complaint after enduring racial discrimination by her white male supervisor and one other supervisor, a white female. When Ms. South was originally interviewed for the job, she reported that at the conclusion of her
first meeting with her supervisor, he "requested" that she complete her
degree, even though the job did not require a degree. After working in this
department for a short time, she discovered that three white women in her
department (one had worked there twenty-seven years, another thirteen
years, and another three years) did not have degrees. Ms. South's duties at
one time included holding down three positions, one of which required a
degree, while one staff member was on sick leave and another was on
maternity leave. When one of the positions for which Ms. South was
backup became vacant, she was not offered the position, even though she
had filled in for the employee who held the position during that
employee's absence. It should be noted that Ms. South, while performing
multiple responsibilities within the university's department, enrolled in

college courses to complete her undergraduate degree. By the time she was interviewed by this author, Ms. South had hired an attorney and had filed an official complaint with the State Division of Human Rights, citing the employer for various violations. Ms. South filed her complaint when she figured out that a computer software product was being misused by her and other staff members and the misuse was known and covered up by her supervisors. Apparently, Ms. South had not been offered training on how to properly use the software, while supervisors had been sent to the software training sessions. Ms. South also observed that another African American woman who was hired by the department was also being victimized by departmental discrimination. Ms. South's white supervisor repeatedly withheld information that pertained to their jobs from both of them. Eventually, Ms. South was excluded from key meetings in a tactic that she felt was designed to diminish her self-esteem and self-worth and to isolate her from the office operations.

Ms. South felt that by keeping her so isolated, the employer was trying to make her quit her job. African American women who are caught up in these types of situations must find ways to deflect these senseless attacks. To control her stress, Ms. South would have long talks with her family members, who encouraged her to cling to her faith in God. She also created a workspace for herself that included happy pictures, soothing music, and plants. Unfortunately, Ms. South developed hypertension.

Similar types of university/college faculty behavior were communicated to me by an African American female faculty member at a Midwestern state university. She stated that, during faculty meetings, other faculty would not support her suggestions; instead, the faculty would wait until her suggestion was made by another nonminority faculty member, and then support it. Then she would say, "Didn't I just make that suggestion?" She resented the fact that the faculty thought she did not know that they were trying to shatter her self-esteem. By speaking up, she removed that burden from her heart and her psyche.

In Scott's (1991) book *The Habit of Surviving,* one of her study subjects, Sara, reports on her ordeal as a teacher. Sara started her academic career as a scientist at a state institution. She soon realized that all the white people in the lab were engaged in the real research while she and two other black females were relegated to doing routine scut work. She left her job in the lab after her son was born and, when she returned to the labor market, took a job in the science department at a local high school. The science department staff primarily consisted of white males. In this position, parents would tell her that their son was doing badly in her class because he had a black teacher.

Considering these situations, it's clear why it is so very important to understand group dynamics, organizational behavior, and old-fashioned, out-of-date racism, African American women must learn the stress busters that help them survive these and other kinds of attacks discussed in this book.

CASE VII: WHITE MALE SUPERVISOR'S RESPONSE TO DIVERSITY: FEDERAL GOVERNMENT

The federal government, which employs more than 275,000 African Americans, is one of the largest employers of African Americans. One of these employees, Marsha Coleman-Adebayo, who worked for the Environmental Protection Agency (EPA), filed a discrimination suit and won $600,000 that was later reduced to $300,000 (the federal government has a cap on awards to government employees). As I explained in chapter 2, stress plays an important role in the development of hypertension. Ms. Coleman-Adebayo may have saved her own life by isolating herself from her office supervisors and office stressors by working from home.

White male privilege was the rule, not the exception before the Civil Rights Act of 1964. Until 1964, "White men in corporations had to compete against only 33 percent of the adult population, according to the U.S. Census of 1970—that was the percentage of the adult U.S. population that was white men. But after 1964, white men, at least by law, had to compete on a more equitable basis with the other 67% as well, i.e. with women and women of color" (Bowser and Hunt 1996, p. 173). In addition to competing with African American women for jobs, white males now had to compete with their own sisters, mothers, and aunts. White males now find themselves facing greater competition in the workplace where "racism and sexism have helped to shield them from the need to test their skills" (Bowser and Hunt 1996, p. 173). As the job market and the economic climate of America continue to deteriorate as a result of the events of September 11, 2001 and the war with Iraq, will racist behavior by employers continue to be a way of American life, or will Americans pull together and abandon racism for good, fulfilling the promise of this great nation where everyone is important, regardless of their racial or cultural differences?

Bernstein (2001, p. 65), in his article "Racism in the Workplace," reported on the results of a *Business Week* investigation over a two-month period into what was labeled as "an extensive pattern of charges of racial hatred in U.S. workplaces . . . nearly four decades after the Civil Rights Acts of 1964." *Business Week* also reported that the Equal Employment Opportunity Commission receives nine thousand complaints a year. Yet racial harassment charges have jumped by 100 percent since 1990, while minority employment has only grown 36 percent. So, I ask you, what is the problem? Is it the unwillingness to share the American dream or simply greed?

African American Women versus African American Men in the Workplace

Black men in America have struggled to remain viable entities in their family, workplace, and community. In the workplace African American men are confronted with decisions (to take sides with administration) that affect their livelihood and their job. Sometimes these decisions can make or break a person. How black men relate to their black sisters is the focus of this section. When I began to gather information for analysis and presentation on the relationship between African American men and women in the workplace, the paucity of studies regarding their workplace relationships was most disturbing. However, there is one very highly publicized black-male-versus-black-female workplace confrontation that I will present. This male-versus-female confrontation has all the ingredients that can provoke stress in the African American female: love, hate, and sexual harassment.

CASE VIII: ANOTHER LOOK AT THE HILL/THOMAS RELATIONSHIP IN THE WORKPLACE AND ANITA'S STRESSORS

In the history of this great nation, there has never been a more highly publicized male-female relationship gone bad than the Anita Hill/ Clarence Thomas affair. The Bill Clinton/Monica Lewinsky affair may have come close; however, the Hill/Thomas affair is relevant to this discussion and African American women. Yes, we may have had enough of both of them, but another look at the Hill/Thomas relationship more than a decade after it came to light and without the media hype can allow us to more fully examine it in the context of this book's framework of stress-provoking incidents. Since this book focuses on how African American women deal with stress that emanates from their relationships, the Hill/Thomas story has particular resonance.

Hill grew up in Lone Tree, Oklahoma, where African Americans are "scarce as hen's teeth." When she left Oklahoma for Yale Law School in 1977, before her twentieth birthday, she left twelve other siblings behind and a mother and father. Her mother was the daughter of a Baptist deacon and farmer, and her father, the son of a farmer. Like most African American parents, Anita's wanted their children to be educated. And Anita, fueled by role models like Yvonne Burke and Patricia Harris, wanted to succeed and make her parents and family proud. Yale, unlike Oklahoma State where she earned her undergraduate degree, was built for young, white, privileged males and had only started admitting women in 1969.

Anita completed her studies, passed the bar, moved to Washington, D.C., and later met Clarence Thomas at a house party in her apartment building, where he was living temporarily, having just separated from his first wife. Thomas, who was waiting for a Reagan administration appointment that he received as Assistant Secretary of Education for Civil Rights, later hired Anita as his assistant. Hill noted some philosophical differences between them, but she worked for him because, as she notes, "He was black [and] was certainly a major factor in my decision to work for him [and] He even spoke of black solidarity" (Hill 1997, p. 61). According to Hill, Thomas required loyalty to his administration; "no one was to be trusted. Because I was one of two personal assistants, I had only one colleague, and he encouraged me not to trust even her." Hill states that, as the personal assistant to the appointee, she was expected to protect him from his higher-ups, as well as from career government workers. "And I was expected to keep Thomas' secrets, personal and work related, no matter how disturbing" (p. 61). In an environment where Hill reported that patronage ruled the work world, if you did not perform, you could be blackballed, fired, or relegated to an irrelevant job. Stress is not mentioned as one of her feelings when she writes, "I balanced my concerns for the issues and my ability to voice objections directly to Thomas against a flawed work environment that I was powerless to change" (p. 62).

In a situation where an employee feels powerless in her nine-to-five job, you have limited options open to you: quit or otherwise remove yourself from the stress. Like other black women who work for black men, there may be some speculation as to whether an African American woman was hired for her ability or instead more for her sex and less for her race. Because of this, Hill states, "[I] stuck to my work, made only a few friends in the office, and kept counsel with friends outside the office about Clarence Thomas" (p. 66). In this somewhat isolated situation, Hill states that she had no romantic relationship with him. She further states, "Thomas began to pressure me to see him socially [she refused; however, he persisted]" (p. 66). Gradually, his confessions about his life became "more graphic, and more vulgar" (p. 69). Dealing with advances from a man with whom you work can be very destructive in a work environment for women in general, and more specifically, for African American women dealing with African American men. Hill, in her statement to the U.S. Senate on September 23, 1991, further details Thomas's advances.

She testified: "Clarence Thomas would call me into his office for reports on education issues and projects or, if his schedule was full of outside appointments, he would suggest that we go to lunch together at one of the area government cafeterias. After a brief discussion about work, he would turn the conversation to discussions about sexual interests. His conversations were very vivid. He spoke about acts that he had seen in pornographic films involving such things as women having sex with animals and films involving group sex and rape scenes" (p. 69). Hill also states that Thomas's advances toward her began to abate when he met a new honey and was about to become the head of EEOC, where he offered Hill a job that she accepted as his assistant until she left in 1983. As Hill testified about these vivid conversations, 30 million Americans were glued to their television sets. What did Anita do to help her alleviate the stress she must have experienced before and during these hearings? From her book *Speaking Truth to Power*, I have selected some of what I believe were her stress busters at that time.

1. "I work hard to forget. I simply convinced myself that what mattered was my right to not cling too tightly to hurt, and to move on with my life" (p. 69). Removal of herself from the stressor.

2. "University of Oklahoma [her employer] was a place where I could be productive and I could make a contribution" (p. 88). Cultivating feelings of self-worth.

3. "My involvement with other law teachers, particularly minority law teachers, was great help for me" (p. 88). Seeking out social support.

4. Returned to an exercise routine, five-mile walks, three times a week before and after the Thomas hearing. Rejuvenation.

5. Confided in a friend her experience with Thomas. Seeking out social support.

6. Attended family Christmas dinner. Seeking out social support.

7. Prayed. Placing her burdens in the hands of the Lord.

8. Received holiday cards and greetings. Seeking out social support.

9. Savored gifts (fruitcake). Seeking out social support.

10. Took trip to San Antonio. Travel.

11. Attended conferences. Seeking out professional support.

12. Quilting. Pursuing a hobby.

13. Journaling. Expressing feelings through words.

Regardless of your personal views about the Hill/Thomas affair, I am sure you will agree that Hill had to experience some enormously stressful encounters with the media cameras in her face at every given opportunity and in questioning from senators, friends, and, especially, her mother and father. I have elected to present some of what I believe were Anita's key stress busters, because, whether consciously or subconsciously, everyone needs stress relievers.

CHAPTER 5

Service and Organizational Membership as a Source of Stress

When African females were brought to America from the west coast of Africa as indentured servants or slaves, they not only brought their weaving and spinning skills, they also carried with them customs and beliefs about village kinship from their ancestral homelands. One of these was the custom of oneness in their approach to family and group relationships. To this end everyone worked to take care of all the members of the families who lived in the community; thus the phrase, "It takes a village to raise a child." These two ethics—the drive to belong, along with the determination to support all the members of the village—undergirded the establishment of African American female-headed service organizations in America.

One of the earliest of these organizations was the National Association of Colored Women Clubs, established in 1896, followed by many others like Alpha Kappa Alpha (AKA). AKA was formed in 1908 by nine female students at Howard University and the membership is now well over 170,000 women in over 900 chapters. Also founded on the Howard University campus was Delta Sigma Theta in 1913. These Delta women pledged themselves to work in the areas of academic excellence and service. In 1938, a group of African American women/mothers formed the organization, Jack and Jill of America, Inc. These women were dedicated to promoting educational and cultural activities for their children; later the group's mission was extended to include offering services to communities through the work of over 20,000 members in 216 chapters.

The Link's, Inc., founded in 1946, is another African American female–headed organization that now has over 270 chapters in forty states and

South Africa. This organization's mission is to serve the community and to serve and support its members. In keeping with the Afrocentric culture and customs of our ancestors, these service organizations were formed to provide a service for their communities. They have kept their commitment to the collective mission and I salute them.

ORGANIZATIONAL STRESSORS AND BELONGING

African American organizations are necessary and supportive; however, when individuals come together under a common banner, there is always the possibility that stressors may develop. All women's organizations set goals and objectives that the membership must strive to achieve. Members may derive a great sense of joy and satisfaction from the work they do; on the other hand, members may encounter a great deal of stress as they work to get the job done.

This chapter will describe the sources of organizational stress that African American women may encounter as members of various groups (not necessarily those just mentioned), and it will suggest ways to buffer your health status from the ill effects of these organizational stressors.

To begin with, African American women must first investigate the goals and objectives of an organization they wish to join. For example, Jack and Jill of America, Inc. is a family organization in which the mother holds the membership, the children participate in various activities, and the mother/child's membership essentially ends when the oldest child graduates from high school. At that point, the majority of these members move on to hold membership in other organizations. As a member of Jack and Jill, an African American woman participates in all meetings and has a voice in setting policies as to how the organization will operate and serve her children. She may also belong to other organizations, such as the Links, Inc., or a sorority, where she is a member for life. When members meet and begin discussing the direction of the group, one member may submit a proposal that does not reflect the child-centered efforts of Jack and Jill. As a result, stress may develop. It is always advisable to clearly understand your role as a member of any group or organization you plan to become associated with.

On the other hand, The Links, Inc., has four major focuses, known as facets, and resources and members' efforts are directed toward their achieving them. Members of the Links chapters are expected to support the organization's facets; the national organization is responsible for providing the leadership and direction that members follow.

Members of an organization who do not support the organization's objectives and leadership direction may find it overwhelming to sit through meetings: their heart rate may increase, and their blood pressure may become elevated when agenda items do not meet with their personal approval. These members can also become the "Members from Hell," and they can create an enormous amount of stress for the organization's leadership and its members. Therefore, the first rule for all African American women who are seeking membership in an organization should be this: *know the organization's goals and objectives before you seek membership,* certainly before paying any dues. Most large African American women's organizations have Web sites that present their history as well as the goals of the organization. Review an organization's goals before you join to make sure you want to belong and to ensure that you can live with the organizational goals.

Another source of organizational stress stems from the failure of the organizational leadership to lead. To explain leadership, I chose a quotation from a female leader whom I admire, Bishop Vashti M. McKenzie. In her book *Leadership Development for Women: Strength in the Struggle* (2001, p. 3) she states, "Leadership is the ability to bring people together for the accomplishment of goals. It is the process that lends the achieving of those goals with the maintenance of the organization." An African American woman who seeks to serve as a leader in an organization must have a leadership style that not only supports the goals of the group but also is exercised fairly throughout the membership. When meeting discussions are nonproductive, the leader must step in and educate the members in order to resolve the issues. She must lead because "leadership has the unique opportunity to create an atmosphere for innovation to take place. A leader can give permission for advancement to take place" (McKenzie 2001, p. 9).

African American women–led organizations that have service among their goals may also raise funds to support their service programs. How funds are used by the organization must be clearly articulated by its leaders or that may cause stress in the organization. Members may also be required to pay dues and then sell tickets for fund-raising events or be assessed a certain amount. A potential source of great stress occurs when the membership does not support the fund-raising efforts or the leadership misuses organization funds. For example, say an organization's fund-raising committee makes its report recommending a particular fund-raiser or a financial assessment for members who don't sell tickets. If you don't support the type of fund-raiser that's been proposed or the financial obligation you must now pay, you may physically experience sweaty hands or an increase in your blood pressure or blood sugar (all of which are detrimental to your health status). If there is an item on the agenda that you know you do not agree with, you have a few options. First, buffer yourself by doing one of the following: do not attend the meeting where funds are discussed; volunteer to serve on the fund-raising committee and make suggestions that can be incorporated into the financial report to the group; go to the meeting and make your concerns known or, more drastically, terminate your membership. I would hope you would not choose to withdraw from the group; however, if you leave meetings with a headache, an upset stomach, heart palpitations, and end up with insomnia, the decision is up to you as to how much you want to sacrifice your well-being and health status.

We freely elect to participate in community organizations, and membership in these groups can give African American women great satisfaction by crediting them for their work. African American women must remember that within an organization's membership may be individuals who bring to meetings their personal life experiences. Some of these experiences may be pleasant; others may make that member the previously mentioned "Member From Hell" or the "Got Ya Member." Leaders must also be aware of the member who may be out to get you, the leader. Yes, to get you. These are members who can create stress for the leader of the organization and for the entire membership. Here are some traits of the "Got Ya Member" in an organization:

1. She will never volunteer for any jobs that will not give her visibility and a forum to speak from.
2. She will talk out of both sides of her mouth and with limited commitment.
3. She will sit in the back of the room during meetings and keep little side conversations going.
4. She will analyze the group membership, looking for the uneducated in terms of the organization's mission so she can elicit their support when needed.
5. Before a meeting she will call the most vocal and venerable members and drop little hints about the failings of the organization leadership.
6. She will make snide comments about the organization's funds. While not quite accusing anyone of misusing funds, she will raise suspicions that the leadership is allowing the misuse of funds. African American women work very hard in service organizations, raising funds and paying dues; they are incensed if anyone suggests that there is any improper use of funds.
7. She is the member who aspires to assume a leadership role but wants to gain power through the back door or an alternate route; this, too, can generate a tremendous amount of stress.
8. She is also the member who is extremely articulate and bright, and knows the rules and regulations of the organization. She is never challenged because she cites "Article 2 section 5"; no one else in the group will have a copy of the bylaws at their fingertips, but she will always carry a copy of the bylaws to every meeting.
9. She is well prepared to challenge the leadership and stress you out.
10. She will also bait other members, goading them into questioning certain policies that cannot be addressed easily by the leader or group. In some cases there is no answer or there are several answers, and she knows it, but she will nonetheless allow the group to fall into a dark hole from which there is no escape.

11. She is also the member who will find alternate routes to destroy the leaders' program.

12. She is someone who will plan her rise to a leadership position years in advance, using whoever she can and stepping on anyone who gets in her way by starting rumors to destroy her competition's reputation. When all is said and done, she may reach her goal to lead some of our African American organizations.

I specified these twelve traits because it is important for an aspiring leader to know where some of her stress originates from and what to do about it. Simply stated, you must know your membership. Build a profile of all vocal members. Recruit a member (an ally) to help you. During meetings, have one of your allies sit near the member you suspect is attempting to rise to power. It's okay to aspire to leadership; it is how you go about it. Have your allies/field soldiers report back to you after the meetings on any rumblings. Also, once you have identified an individual who is a self-proclaimed rising leader, give her a job. Make her appointment at a meeting so she can't back out. You must, however, give her a responsibility that is both challenging and important. After all, African American leaders should do succession planning and mentor those women who can become leaders through the front door, if you will, rather than through the back door, creating a stress-provoking avenue. And, finally, always appoint a parliamentarian, a Seargent-at-Arms, and be sure to take a copy of your organization's rules/regulations and bylaws with you to all meetings. You must be prepared. And when all seems bleak and out of control, call on the Almighty, for He is always listening.

There is another group of members, the "Lifers," who may also create organizational stress as a result of menopause, PMS, postpartum depression, mental illness, dementia, depression, or substance abuse, just to mention a few health problems. Illnesses can affect all of us, and we must protect our sisters from hurt and pain that others may be experiencing from an illness. Inappropriate behavior and comments made by these members during meetings may be related to the symptoms of the psychological or physiological conditions that they may be suffering from. Sometimes the member is unaware of the effect of her behavior and the leadership must step in to offer a solution and guidance. This is important because sometimes we use the "she-thing" when members step out of the role we have placed them in. As McKenzie (2001, p. 117) explains, we use that "she-thing" (who do she think she is?). "We assign places to one another and we expect them to stay within these boundaries." We must be careful when our sisters in these organizations begin to feel the effects of the aging process. If the leadership fails to act and control their behavior, this can become a source of stress for all members. Members who are

unable to cope with the behavior of other ill members may find it necessary to take a leave or resign altogether. If this happens, the organization
loses those members' talents and is left with an abundance of members
who may exacerbate the stressful organizational environment. We must
stand at attention and answer the call of our sisters. We can't expect those
who hold life membership in some organizations (the Lifers) to leave
when they become ill. It's not sisterly, but we must put in place a mechanism to help them live out their membership term while at the same time
limiting the stressors they cause, which affect the organization as a whole.

African American communities throughout this nation benefit from the
millions in funds and services poured into their communities from The
Links, Inc., Jack and Jill of America, Inc., the Eastern Star, Daughters of
Isis, Delta, AKA, and many other African American women's organizations too numerous to list. However, the members of these organizations
must also realize that participating in some groups may become a source
of stress, and they must find ways to shield themselves from stressors that
may come from organizational participation.

PART II

Stressproof Your Life

Like so many African American women, I wear many hats—professional, mom, sister, grandmother, cook, chauffeur, volunteer, professor, scholar, club member, and author. In addition, I have held several elected positions. At the time of this writing, my son was applying to medical school and my mother was receiving daily radiation treatments for a rare form of esophageal cancer. Every hat an African American woman wears has the potential to create stress, and she must be prepared to handle it. Before I begin to share with you some of the ways to deal with stress, we must first rule out any physical abnormalities that may affect your life expectancy, a life expectancy that is far shorter than that of our white counterparts.

We have learned that the number-one killer of women is heart disease; it kills more women than breast cancer. What is so problematic about this disease is that the symptoms women experience are somewhat different than those experienced by men, so by the time a woman is diagnosed with heart disease, she may have already suffered some heart damage. It's very important, therefore, that women get tested for possible heart disease. One of the basic diagnostic tests is the Stress Test. One of the simplest tests, this is usually covered by health insurance policies. My physician ordered the Cardio-Lite Stress Test. You may have to convince your physician that you need the test if you haven't experienced palpitations or if you don't have a family history of heart disease (check your managed health care or insurance regulations). Once the physician orders the stress test, you will call the hospital and set up an appointment. On the day of the appointment, you will fast (with the exception of water), wear loose clothing and sneakers, and report to the Stress Lab where your physician will be waiting. A technician will place twelve cardiac monitoring leads on your chest and ankles. The cardiac leads are attached to an EKG monitor and your physician will start an intravenous (IV) line. The technician will take your blood pressure (baseline reading) and you will be instructed by your physician to walk on a treadmill, where the speed is periodically increased, while your physician takes your blood pressure reading and injects a medication into your IV while keeping a watchful eye on the EKG. Once the test is over, the cardiac monitoring leads are removed and you will be instructed to eat something fatty and report to the x-ray department. In the x-ray department, a series of films are taken by a gamma camera (a huge machine) that moves very slowly down your body (it does not touch you) while you hold your arms over your head. The technician will instruct you to return the following day for part two of the stress test. The second day you will report to the x-ray department, where you will be given an injection of a dye and additional x-rays will be taken. Your doctor will review the x-ray films for any abnormalities. I was given a Heart Health Status Report. Now that I know that I am "heart healthy," I must work on staying that way. This stress test is a noninvasive diagnostic test and it is well worth the time. Some stress tests may vary from this procedure; however, the objective is the same—to rule out heart disease.

There are many approaches to treating stress-related illnesses and stress in general. They may utilize the medical model as well as alternative approaches. In this part, I will offer many "stress busters" that reduce the stress in your life. Remember that these are only suggestions and are not meant to replace any treatment modality prescribed by your physician or health practitioner. Rather, they are suggestions that may help you deal with the daily struggles associated with a stressful life. I have included the stress busters that I believe African American women will practice and ones that will provide benefits from continued practice. In addition, they could increase your longevity!

CHAPTER 6

Sisters in Motion: Getting Started with the Least Effort

DANCING THE NIGHT AWAY WHILE LISTENING TO YOUR FAVORITE MUSIC

The first stress buster, an African American cultural mainstay, is dancing. Dancing can be very therapeutic. When African slaves were first brought to this country, they were not allowed to carry any of their personal belongings. They did, however, bring their skills, such as carpentry, African drumming, and tribal dancing. Dancing has been, and still remains, African American women's favorite pastime. Dance can be whatever you want it to be with impromptu steps or organized line dancing (e.g., the Electric Slide or the Bus Stop). We can express how we feel in our movements by "Twisting the Night Away." As we immerse ourselves into the music and think about our next step, we move and release the stress in our shoulders and hands while popping our fingers, undulating the stomach, shaking the hips, and moving the legs to the sound and beat of the music. Stress seems to melt away. It's enjoyable and revitalizing. We let our head move forward and back as we wiggle and sashay across the floor. If we have a dance partner, a special honey, a husband, or a significant other, we can inject some romance into our dance ritual. But let's not forget the kids; they can dance with you and this will help to relieve all the family stressors. The residual benefits are many. If "done for just an hour, [the leisurely box step] will burn just over 200 calories for a 150-lb. woman, and if you kick that up a notch and start doing the twist or La Bamba, you can burn three times that amount" (*Prevention's Healing with Motion* 1999, p. 96). Dancing also helps to connect us to ourselves and, as such, relieves loneliness and shields us from depression.

When we surrender to the spirit in church and begin the Holy Ghost dance while speaking in tongues, the gospel brings us another stress buster. Our new age and order of church services now finds the minister and choir being led into a sanctuary of the church by a group of church dancers. While others in the congregation clap their hands and move their feet to the sound of an old Negro spiritual, we feel energized and relieved—free of stress. There are some religions where members of the church will run up and down the church aisles, singing and releasing those pent-up feelings, while they succumb to the gospel. All of this soul-steering, music-driven dance and movement help to bring us closer to our God while it calms our hearts, lifts our spirits, and relieves our stress.

In order to perform the *Dance De-Stressor*, all you need is some good music by artists like the Whispers; the Ojays; Tina Turner; Patty Labelle; Diane Reeves; Roberta Flack; Earth, Wind and Fire; or my favorite song, "The Shadow of Your Smile," performed by the late Herman Fisher of Buffalo, New York. The music must have a strong rhythmic pulse. How long you dance will depend on several factors, such as how tired you are, or how much stress needs to be released.

Music is an important part of African American culture. Like dance, the rhythm brought to America is still with us. For music to work as a de-stressor, it must be mood-altering. Music can get under your skin and send chills up your spine. Because it can provoke so many emotions that affect our mood, music as a stress buster helps African American women connect to better days in the past. And when we connect to the good old days through our favorite tunes, it can transport us back to happier times.

When you combine dance with visual imagery, it can be a powerful stress buster. The residual effects are many. One in particular that is most important is the soothing effect it can have on your blood pressure by reducing the stress hormone cortisol, while increasing the level of stress-relieving endorphins. Don Campbell, author of *The Mozart Effect* (1997), feels that some of Mozart's music can have a positive effect on the emotions.

Now that you are dancing and listening to some great music, let's sing along. What better way to release some of that stress than by singing in the shower? Even if you can't carry a tune, the bathroom echo makes you sound as good as some of those girl groups from the '60s you listen to in the car. Sing in the morning shower and in the car on your way to work. Never mind the person in the next car. You sound good and you are belting out all of that stress before you start your workday. Musicologist and author Elizabeth Miles (1997), in her book *Tune Your Brain: Using Music to Manage Your Mind, Body and Mood,* describes several types of mood music. Music to energize is hip-hop and rock; music to relax is jazz and vocal; music to focus is classical; and "America" by Whitney Houston, tunes sung by Kathy Bowman, First Lady of Antioch Fire Baptist Church, of Buffalo, New York, and "Psalm 23," played by harpist Jeff Majors, are all uplifting. Each of these types of songs/music is within our reach. After a deplorable workday, music can offer you several ways to unwind and reinvigorate yourself. To relax, put on the Whispers, Peabo Bryson, Luther Vandross, Freddy Jackson, or Brian McKnight; to strengthen your concentration, choose something by Kenny G or Mozart; to give yourself a lift, consider Mary J. Bligh's "No More Drama" or Gloria Gaynor's "I Will Survive." When we listen to our favorite music, we reach deep down into our souls and this relieves stress. Music as a stress buster can help those who find it hard to get in touch with their emotions. Music can evoke intense feelings, infusing us with a sense of exhilaration, relaxation, excitement, sadness, or joy. It may also simply help us get in touch with ourselves.

Valada S. Flewellyn (1990) captures the importance of music and dance in the following poem:

TO DANCE

My people love to dance—
  Why shouldn't we?
My people got rhythm;
My people got soul;
We've got a spirit that's hard to hold.
My people can survive in any town;
My people have always been around;
My people love to dance.
We make music;
And it moves us . . .
It Moves Us to Move!
The rhythm is with us . . . always—
Don't fight it . . . Just let go!
You don't have to learn it;
  You just know.
My people love—
My people love . . . people.
My people love
My people love
My people love to
DANCE, DANCE, DANCE, DANCE,
DANCE, DANCE . . . . . .
Dance!

In this poem from *Poetically Just Us* (1990), Flewellyn captures how integral dance is to the African American community. I have discussed how dance and music can be valuable stress busters for stressed-out African American women. Now take Flewellyn's advice and dance, dance, dance!

Our next stress buster takes it to the next level where you can find some of the most energizing movements—walking, jogging, and skipping.

WALKING, JOGGING, AND SKIPPING

One of the most beneficial and totally cost-free exercises is walking. If you're a beginner, stretch and begin walking slowly, then add a little pep to your walk. This gets your heart rate up. In the park, listen to the birds, feel the wind on your face, take a few deep breaths, and blow those stress bubbles away. Walk for five or ten minutes, then rest. Start again. Now let your body tell you how far you want to venture. If you have a dog, walk the dog. Dogs tend to lift our spirits. They can help you pace yourself and also add a measure of protection if you are an evening walker. The benefits of walking are many; however, one of the most significant is the benefit to your heart. The authors of the nurses' health study suggest that "a regimen of brisk walking for 3 or more hours per week could reduce the risk of coronary events in women by 35 to 40% . . . and even 1 hour of walking per week was found to predict a lower risk of coronary heart disease" (Manson, Shlepak, and Wenger 2001, p. 39). There are many benefits from walking. Dr. Michael Cohen, director of Project Nature, states that spending time outdoors can be a mood booster for your endorphins, it can help you shed a few pounds, and it helps to maintain your weight (*Prevention's Healing with Motion* 1999, p. 98). Also, "one study found that women who spend just three hours a week walking at a moderate three miles per hour are less likely to have heart attacks or strokes" (*Prevention's Healing with Motion* 1999, p. 405). Walking also helps your heart to beat and work harder, thus making it stronger. In addition, it lowers your blood pressure while boosting levels of good cholesterol in your bloodstream. Walking also strengthens leg muscles and lubricates joints.

Once you have gotten your pace up, you are ready to add jogging to your exercise routine. I suggest that, before you jog, you make sure that you have the correct walking or jogging sneakers. This will save wear and tear on your knees, your feet, and your toes. If you have managed to incorporate these exercises into your routine, let's take it one step further—skipping.

Skipping is not a new pastime but it's a very interesting way to burn calories and release stress. By incorporating intervals of skipping into your walking and jogging regimen, it breaks up the exercise routine and makes it a fun workout. Skipping, once you get over the embarrassment of this wonderful exercise, is reported to be less stressful on joints and to burn more calories than running. Because most girls learn to skip when they are young, we automatically revert back to those good old days. Yes, it will alter how we feel; it is a distinct mood lifter. Try skipping when you feel down. Once you decide to take up skipping, remember all the safety tips. Check out the web for skipping leaders and skipping clubs in your area. Happy skipping!

Next let's turn our attention to a stress buster that is not so strenuous; however, it requires equally strong legs and feet, a sense of coordination, and the ability to point in the right direction. I am thrilled to introduce you to or reacquaint you with the wonderful world of golfing, our next stress buster. And I applaud and encourage those who are already easing stress out on the links.

SWING AND PING—THE SOUNDS WE LIKE TO HEAR: GOLF

Golfing was one of the African American community's favorite recreational sports long before Tiger Woods was conceived. It's hard to believe that most Americans attribute African Americans' interest in golf to this young man. Tiger, of course, has made his mark; however, many African Americans paved the way for him, making his life on the fairway much more bearable than it might have been otherwise and easing the way for him to compete in the prestigious Master's Tournament.

In their book, *African American Golfers during Jim Crow Era*, authors Marvin P. Dawkins and Graham C. Kinlock (2000) point out that the African American golfers of the 1920s learned the sport by caddying for white golfers on segregated golf courses. The next three decades would see a tremendous change in who was found on the golf course. Thirteen African American women, led by Helen Webb Harris, the wife of a physician, spearheaded efforts to integrate the golf courses of America. The Wake Royal Golf Club (founded in 1936 in Philadelphia) had three objectives: to cultivate golf as a pastime among African American women, to make potential players into champions, and to make a permanent place for African American women in the world of golf. These women went on to become some of the earliest activists, helping to pave the way for thousands of African American women's golf clubs. One such club, the Divot Divas of Atlanta, Georgia, was founded by Bernadette Carter-Jones in 1997 after the death of her eighteen-year-old son, Louis C. Hudson. When her son passed away on Valentine's Day 1996, she spent more than eight months alone. During this protracted period of grief-stricken solitude, she would take to the golf course to be alone where she, her son, and her daughter had golfed as a family. After this very difficult period, some close friends encouraged her to organize a club, so she organized the Divot Divas' Golf Group. The group's membership includes some of Atlanta's top African American women executives, who take to the course the second Wednesday of each month. It is a friendship golf group without the competitive edge. Members play golf, have lunch or dinner, and once a year they travel to renowned golf resorts in Hilton Head, Jamaica, or West Palm Beach.

Figure 6.1 Divot Divas' Golf Group: (top to bottom, L–R) Marvey Walker, Karen Webster, Valerie Golston, Monica Kaufman, Mary Robinson, Deborah Lyn-Patrick, Pamela Hoffman, Bernadette Carter-Jones (founder), Cheryl Dixon. (Not pictured: Delores Crockett, LaJean Gould, Sonjia Young, Mary Teamen.)

Not only are there psychological benefits to golfing, but there are physical ones as well that come from twisting the torso while working your shoulders, arms, and thigh muscles. In addition, walking the golf course helps you shed a few unwanted pounds and firm up those gluteus maximus (buttocks) muscles. Remember, golfing is a fun exercise and you must struggle to keep it from becoming a stressor. While on the course, smell the fresh air, look at the blue skies, and feel the warm sun on your face. Your mind will be relieved by your concentration on the weather rather than on your next swing. Thousands of African American women turn off cell phones and pagers to hit the links, like the Divot Divas' of Atlanta; the young African American golfer, Angel Mimes, a member of the Jackson State Golf team; and professional LPGA golfer Renee Powell. Golfing is one of the most prized forms of working out and a super stress buster. I love the game, but, like so many sisters, I have scheduling problems that can make you lose your swing. I have made myself a promise to do better. How about you?

PUMPING UP THE EFFORT: TAKING IT TO THE NEXT LEVEL

Bicycling

Bicycling can be an excellent form of exercise, a real adventure, and a way to meet others. The residual benefits are that it reduces stress levels and helps you shed a few unwanted pounds as well as keeping those buttocks muscles firm. Also, while you're exploring the neighborhood or the bike path at the local university, as I do, your mind begins to float, and pent-up stress vanishes as your blood pressure begins to go down. Yes, bicycling lowers your blood pressure. In addition, when you lose weight, your blood pressure drops. This is supported by the American Heart Association, which reports that "a 150 pound person can burn up to 240 calories an hour while cycling at just 6 miles per hour" (Booker 2001, p. 88). When you cycle, you work your leg and buttocks muscles and firm up overall, which gives you a sleek and slimmer appearance. With strong leg muscles, the added benefit is strengthened joints, which in turn helps to prevent wear and tear on hip muscles, thereby preventing osteoarthritis. Sisters: invest in a bike! There are many kinds of bikes on the market. And don't forget a helmet.

Bicycling will also increase your need for fluids and will help to promote the need to drink eight glasses of water a day. Further, perspiration from cycling will open your pores, eliminating bodily impurities and keeping your pores from clogging up and causing those dread pimples/breakouts. You will breathe deeply, too, and this expands your lung capacity. This will help when you participate in jogging and aerobic classes: you won't tire out as easily. So put on your headphones and your favorite music (you must be cautious so use one ear piece so you can hear traffic) and let bicycling relieve stress. It has done that for me. Also, it's the kind of stress buster you can do alone or with your husband/boyfriend or with your children. You can make the ride a family affair, especially when there is some family friction. Ride it off. When you come home from a long ride, the problem may not seem so challenging; it may have lost its importance. Whatever happens, remember that you are trying to relieve your pent-up stress, not to give some family member a chance to dump another problem in your lap. And, when the family stops to rest, make sure it's near an ice-cream parlor! You can have some low-calorie frozen yogurt and you'll ride the calories off before you get home. At the same time, the family will be so busy trying to decide on the ice-cream flavor that family squabbles may just disappear. If you're not adventurous and not willing to explore a bike trail in your neighborhood or on the campus of your local college, try a spinning class in a local health club. There are over three thousand fitness centers in America. Whatever you choose, don't forget safety, especially when bicycling. Keep the volume down on your Walkman, watch for moving vehicles, and if you are on dimly lit roads or paths, be alert to your surroundings, especially if you are alone. Now let's speed up the next activity with a tennis racket—our next stress buster.

Tennis

When Venus and Serena Williams hit the tennis courts, everyone took notice, not because they were phenomenal tennis players, but because they had strong and shapely bodies. They were healthy and they played well. African American women have been playing tennis for years, mostly for the fun of the sport and for the physical benefits from the running and stretching of leg and arm muscles. Deep breathing from the running helps to cleanse the lungs of carbon dioxide and perspiration opens the sweat glands to release impurities from the body. Also, serving the ball makes you stretch and twist your torso. Since tennis is played with a partner, you are more apt to keep up this form of exercise. Don't worry about keeping score; just have fun. When you have mastered the sport, then you can keep score, unless you just enjoy the exercise and don't care about scoring. Tennis requires good sneakers and loose-fitting clothing

Roller-Skating

One of my favorite exercises is roller-skating. This form of exercise can also burn calories. Roller-skating was very popular in the 1950s, with Roller Jam and Roller Derby where skaters would whiz by at speeds over thirty-five miles an hour. Teams of coeds would team up and win prizes. However, it's not about the prize; it's about how it makes you feel to escape into a different thought process, relieving some of that pent-up stress. Take a few minutes to investigate where in your neighborhood you can take lessons. Roller blades may be a little more difficult to master without lessons.

Whatever stress buster you choose, try to remember that they are offered to help keep you on this earth. Far too many of our sisters are leading sedentary lifestyles, sliding from office chair to dinner chair to their favorite TV chair/couch, and this is killing us.

After dinner, wash the dishes (no, do not use the dishwasher), scrub the kitchen floor (burn up those dinner calories), now take out the garbage, and take a walk. Each of these post-dinner activities will keep your dinner from settling around your middle and your hips. As you will see from the next chapter, your body responds to what your mind tells it to do. So tell your body to dance, jog, skip, or just take a walk—moving right along, sisters.

CHAPTER 7

Mind Over Matter, Sisters

"It is the mind that makes the body."

—Sojourner Truth

LEARN TO BREATHE THE RIGHT WAY AND BLOW THOSE BLUES AWAY

Anxiety and stress tend to make us breathe more slowly and more shallowly. Before we can move into the next set of stress-busting exercises, we must learn to breathe correctly. I know you are probably saying to yourself, "I'm breathing just fine or I would die." Not necessarily. You breathe in oxygen and exhale the waste, carbon dioxide. When you are breathing deeply, this triggers a relaxation response from the parasympathetic nervous system.

Breathing correctly can divert your attention away from the stressor and, as you begin to concentrate on your breathing, stress begins to flow away with each breath.

Deep breathing exercises are taught preoperatively to patients who will be given general anesthesia (put to sleep). It is the deep breathing technique that helps the postoperative patients keep air flowing through their lungs and that helps to loosen congestion, which, if not removed from the lungs following surgery, could cause pneumonia. The benefits of deep breathing outweigh the time spent incorporating them into a relaxation program. The book, *How to Stay Healthy the Natural Way* (Guinness 1993, p. 109), presents the following very easy-to-follow steps to deep breathing.

Taking a Deep Breath

- Sit upright or lie supine in a relaxed position with your spine straight.
- Breathe in slowly through your nose and imagine that you are pushing air deep into your abdomen.
- Note how your abdomen expands and rises as the lungs fill with air.
- Breathe out slowly through your nose, contracting your abdominal muscles to press the diaphragm up and push the air out of your lungs.
- Continue breathing in this way, watching how your abdomen rises and falls.

Also, if you are having trouble losing weight, it could be due to incorrect breathing. A 1997 study by the International Breath Institute says that "when excess fat is accumulated, it's the result of hydrogen built up. Only when the body gets enough oxygen can that hydrogen burn and turn into energy" ("Breathe Away Fat" 1997, p. 22). You can then take this energy and walk a mile.

Now that you have learned to relax and breathe correctly, you can move to the next technique that will help you to de-stress.

RELAXATION

Before your body can begin to heal and mend the damage that has been caused by stress, you must learn how to relax. Sometimes this is easier said than done. Relaxing has been shown to aid patients who suffer from chronic illnesses, like diabetes, or acute illnesses, like heart disease, and remains one of the least costly ways to help you manage your stress. Relaxation is so important that it is being taught to those who are really trying to control life stressors. In fact, at the Mind and Body Institute, Dr. Herbert Benson teaches his techniques to patients and caregivers. Dr. Benson has students at the Institute practice these techniques at least twice a day for ten to twenty minutes. His seven basic techniques are very easy to follow and are offered here for inclusion in your own "Stress Reduction Contract for Life" (see chapter 9).

1. Find a very quiet room (no phones, TV, or people noises).
2. Choose a word or phrase to focus your attention on. Once selected do not change it. This word or sound will help to trigger your relaxation response.
3. Sit with your back straight, hands resting in your lap.
4. Close your eyes and take a few breaths.
5. Breathe normally, slowly but rhythmically. Be aware of your breath and repeat your focus word on each exhalation.
6. Clear your mind; don't let any unpleasant thoughts distract you.
7. Continue for ten to twenty minutes, if possible. When time is up, stay quiet for a few more minutes.

There are a number of relaxation techniques like Dr. Benson's. Regardless of which technique you choose, this is a noninvasive technique and must be practiced, but it is very easy to learn. My personal technique includes all of Dr. Benson's with one addition—I include visualization (discussed later in this chapter).

Relaxation is so important to health maintenance that health spas have begun to hire trained consultants who spend time with clients who are interested in learning relaxation techniques. The next stress buster is a little more technical and requires your honest commitment.

BIOFEEDBACK

When I began to decide what stress busters African American women would be more apt to adopt, biofeedback was not at the top of my list. However, as I investigated the benefits, it was clear that, if practiced correctly, it would make us pay closer attention to our bodies. Through our participation in biofeedback, we get connected to a technique that can help shield us from daily stressors. I was a little leery about presenting biofeedback because it takes time to learn the technique—and time is something lacking in most African American women's schedules. As LaGina Adams states in her article in *Black Enterprise* "More Work and Less Pay" (2001, p. 42), "from 1989 to 1998 the average middle-class white family increased its work hours by 238, averaging a total of 3,789 hours per year where middle-class African American families worked an average of 4,278 hours per year, approximately 500 hours more than whites." Much of this increase is not in one nine-to-five job but rather with a second part- or full-time job. African Americans are, therefore, overworking themselves just to keep up, exposing themselves to the related stress and anxiety that increase our risk of heart disease, stroke, and hypertension. Combating these risks is a major reason that you must learn and use stress busters.

Biofeedback is safe and noninvasive, but it does require that you learn your body's signals through self-assessment and self-control. With a therapist trained to help individuals under stress, you learn to control your body's response as you move from a stressed state to a de-stressed state. While observing your physiological responses (muscle tension, skin temperature) recorded on a sensory monitor, you are trained to make more positive bodily adjustments. For example, "You can change the temperature in one hand as compared to the other" (Edlin, Golanty, and Brown 1996, p. 24) or alleviate a series of other complaints, as in the following list (p. 119):

Biofeedback Treatment of Diseases
- Tension Headache
- Migraine Headache
- Hypertension

- Insomnia
- Muscle Tension
- Anxiety
- Panic Attack
- Stress Incontinence

There are other types of body-sensing devices, like the mood ring of the 1970s and the bio-dot ruler of the 1990s. Both of these measure body temperature. If the mood ring stays blue, it means that you are relaxed, and not under any stress. The bio-dot ruler works by placing your thumb and forefinger on a black dot, holding it for fifteen seconds, then reading a scale. If the dot turns blue, you are calm; if it turns green, you are normal; if it turns red you are experiencing tension; if it turns black, you are under stress. The creator of the bio-dot ruler, Bob Grabbain, also relies on his invention. He states, "I learned long ago to breathe deeply and to get my blood flowing by practicing relaxation" (*Prevention's Healing with Motion* 1999, p. 45).

As previously mentioned, biofeedback might not be for everyone. I also suggest that if you use any methods presented here and you're under a doctor's/health practitioner's care, you should be sure your doctor is aware that you are practicing the technique.

MEDITATION

Once you have found that relaxation can help relieve some of your stress, it's time to take your thinking to another level. It's time to incorporate the benefits of meditation into your relaxation program. The "beneficial effects of meditation are similar to those of deep relaxation, but with one additional reward of facilitating communication with the spiritual aspect of our being" (Wildwood 1997, p. 22). There are many approaches to meditation and whichever you choose it's up to you. What I share here is what I feel to be important aspects that we must use to de-stress ourselves. We must find ways to clear from our minds the daily bombardment of negative stimuli. We must quiet our thoughts. I find that lying down helps me to relax (although some believe that position makes you drift off and fall asleep). Others prefer to sit upright on the floor with their legs in a crossed position; still others sit at a table or a desk, or in a rocking chair. Remember Tina Turner's movie, *What's Love Got to Do With It?* Before each performance or after her husband abused her, Tina Turner would sit at a table, recite a mantra, and meditate. I prefer to meditate at night before I go to sleep. However, the place you select to meditate should be comfortable, and you should try to train your mind to meditate. If possible, you should meditate at the same time and in the same place every day. That's why at night, before I go to sleep, I am able to clear my mind and meditate. I find it easy at that time of day to flow into an altered state of consciousness. Since September 11 and the wars in Afghanistan and Iraq, I find that meditation and prayer are effective techniques to block out some of the daily office discussion, and the television and radio accounts of these national tragedies. There are others who strongly believe that meditation should be done first thing in the morning, before the mind is cluttered and before the hassles of the day begin. Still others believe that meditation is most easily accomplished at sunset. You are the best judge of what works for you, but once you have found the right time and place and have rid yourself of distractions, noise will not affect you while you ease your mind into a state of meditation.

Although not essential for meditation, a warm room that is well venti-lated and one that contains a focal point like a picture or object, such as a crystal, enhance the effects of meditation. These are suggestions and tech-niques that have worked for me. What works for one person may not work for another. You must find your own niche. If you meditate for ten to fifteen minutes a day, it will help to refresh your mind, reducing stress while enhancing your well-being. In 1995 and 1993, I had two difficult losses—the death of both my husband and my brother. And while I was editing this book, my mother passed away. Meditation would have been very difficult for me if I hadn't already incorporated this technique into my lifestyle. During this time I found that one other technique helped dis-pel negative thoughts, those thoughts that creep into your psyche and eat away at your deepest sense of self-worth: reading an inspirational piece. For me it was Susan Taylor's book, *In The Spirit* (1993). Her writing style and the flow of her words captured my thoughts, lifted my spirits, and prepared me for meditation.

Some people like to recite a mantra that prepares their mind for medi-tation. As previously mentioned, in the movie *What's Love Got to Do With It?*, Tina Turner, a battered wife, meditated and recited "Om Mani Padome Hum." As we know from this film, Tina Turner became so depressed that she took more than fifty tranquilizers, in an unsuccessful attempt to end her life. It was the power she received through meditation, where she found solace, that she learned to cope with the physical and mental abuse inflicted on her by her husband. The Buddhist chant that Tina used has a rolling rhythm that moves you along. Buddhists have used meditation for centuries to find inner peace. We cannot dismiss meditation as the practice of an Eastern religion that has no real benefits, because "meditation has been successful in the treatment of high blood pressure, heart disease, migraine headaches, and autoimmune diseases such as diabetes and arthritis. It has proved helpful in curtailing obses-sive thinking, anxiety, depression and hostility" (Davis, Eshelman, and McKay 1995, p. 41). Meditation has been shown to decrease the level of lactic acid in the blood, which is thought to be associated with anxiety.

Speaking from personal experience, I know that stressful life events that are out of your control can damage your physical health, but meditation can help. Prior to an anticipated stressful life event, I used meditation and mind sweeping (like taking a broom or vacuum cleaner to your brain and sucking out all bad thoughts) to get rid of negative thoughts; without these techniques I would not have been able to survive the stressors that event unleashed. For weeks prior to the event, I meditated and prayed to ease all subconscious negative thoughts. At the time of the actual event, the mind sweep process that controlled my thinking helped to buffer the effects of the stressors. In fact, there were times I actually meditated in a crowd. You may refer to this process as "tuning them out" or "turning them off" and turning on meditation. Whatever you choose to believe, meditation helped me. Meditation is simply a way to train the mind to cooperate with you and your demands. That is, when you want the world to stop messing with you, you tell your mind that now it's time to take me to a more pleasant place. The following is a quick guide to meditation for beginners.

Quick Guide

1. Find a quiet place.
2. Sit up straight with back support.
3. Close your eyes.
4. Loosen tight clothing and relax your muscles.
5. Be mindful of your breathing.
6. Chant.
7. Practice, practice once a day for 10–20 minutes.

Meditation can be one of your most valuable allies when you feel yourself drifting into a negative frame of mind.

THE POWER OF PRAYER

Prayer is a powerful weapon against stress. Prayer can take you where you want to go and keep you there. In her book *Too Blessed to Be Stressed*, Susan J. Cook (1998, p. 11) states that "Stress is a distraction that keeps me from fulfilling God's call on my life." She notes that even though we may not be full-time ministers ourselves, the same thing applies to each of us. It is important that we keep stress from destroying our peace of mind. For, as I have previously stated, the mind can be trained to respond to what you tell it to do. As stress attempted to creep into my mind during a recent national organization's convention, I had to keep reminding my mind that I wanted the energy to reflect God's will and not women's and that only through my connection to God through prayer do I survive.

Among the studies that attribute improved health to off-site or remote intercessory prayers, Adler (1999) found that nine hundred patients admitted to a coronary care unit who were prayed for got better. Further, some research has shown that African Americans read the Bible, attend religious services, and pray on a regular basis more than their white counterparts (Hirch, Kent, and Silverman 1972). I believe that prayer has been our salvation, African Americans' sustaining power, the key to our overall survival in a hostile and sometimes unpleasant land. As bell hooks (2001, p. 95) notes in her book *Salvation,* "Prayer along with religious belief allowed enslaved black females to develop an oppositional spirit where they were able to resist seeing themselves through the eyes of their oppressor." Church is one of the oldest African American institutions and has always offered a sanctuary for African American women who needed a safe haven not only to protect their spirit but also to talk to God and send their prayers forward. Each time the minister begins to preach about something that touches our inner feelings, we say *Amen.* Each *Amen* releases a little of that stress and turns our thoughts toward a calm and welcoming mind-set—that of the Almighty. Every day African American women turn their attention to God starting with a prayer breakfast, or call a prayer line like "Silent Unity" (my favorite prayer line), or before they have their hair done. These behaviors have stress-buffering properties— they take your psychic energy and place it into the framework of God's contextual help, if you will.

Prayer is the one way you can create a pleasant state of mind. Regardless of your organized religion, prayer can relieve your stress. Meditation can be a form of praying. That's okay as long as the end result is the release of stress. The release of stress is very important, as noted in a study by Krause and Van Tran (1989, p. 14), which showed that while "stress tended to erode feelings of self worth and mastery, this negative affect was offset or counterbalanced by increased religious involvement." And further, when interviewed on the *Today* show, Dr. Harry Cohen (2002) stated that research has shown that people who pray have less stress, as well as adding up to seven years to their lives. You see, when we pray we are having a mental conversation with God and we are telling Him how we feel when we are asking for help. We really don't have to ask for help because God knows why we are calling on Him. For the prayer process to be successful, you must believe that He is hearing you and that your prayers will be answered.

When I have been under a great deal of pressure or know that a stressful event is about to occur, I enter into a perceptual prayer state of mind with the Creator. When I pray, I ask not only for personal help but also help for family and friends or whoever I think needs a Prayer Booster. Today it is the Reverend Jesse Jackson; Luther Vandross; Janice Marie Scott, a victim of the September 11 attacks (see Epilog); my late mother; and all the victims of 9/11 and the war with Iraq.

African American women must keep those old Negro spirituals close to heart when stress comes creeping into their lives, spirituals like "Lay Your Burdens Down." While attending church services at Israel United Methodist Church in Albany, New York, in 2001, I read in the bulletin the following communication from God:

TO ALL WHO BELIEVE IN ME

Good Morning!

I am God. Today I will be handling all of your problems. Please remember that I do not need your Help. If the devil happens to deliver a situation to you that you cannot handle, do not attempt to resolve it. Kindly put it in the SFJTD (something for Jesus to do) box. It will be addressed in My time, not yours. Once the matter is placed into the box, do not hold onto it or attempt to remove it. Holding on or removal will delay the resolution of your problem. If it is a situation that you think you are capable of handling, please consult me in prayer to be sure that it is the proper solution. Because I do not sleep or slumber, there is no need for you to lose any sleep. Rest, my child. If you need to contact me, I am only a prayer away. As with all good things, Please pass this on.

Love, God

We walk by faith, not by sight, and when we pray and ask the Lord for help, we must believe He will answer.

Taking our faith to the next level we must shake off those evil thoughts so we can learn to love and help each other. Our next mental exercise will banish those negative spirits.

DE-GRUDGE YOUR MIND

Before we can achieve complete relaxation, we must get rid of those negative thoughts or grudges we are harboring. I know this is easier said than done, but we must face the reality of grudges: they can tear you apart and those around you as well. A study by the Society for Behavioral Medicine found that "forgiveness helped to lower blood pressure and reduce tension, stress and even anxiety" (Bolden 1999, p. 86). In fact, this study also revealed that women were less forgiving than men. I know this is true because in my own family, I have relatives who stopped speaking for years over something so minor it's not worth mentioning here. There are some of you out there still holding grudges since kindergarten. When these grudges are held for long periods of time, each time you see the person, you're reminded of the grudge and your stomach begins to boil. This makes stomach acids flow and those acids eat away your stomach lining and produce stomach ulcers. And for what?

In the book *Mother Love's "Forgive or Forget: Never Underestimate the Power of Forgiveness,"* (Bolden 1999), Tonya Bolden lists the following steps to forgiveness for healing those old wounds:

- Acknowledge that a wrong has been done.
- When you're asking for forgiveness, give the person you offended time.
- Don't be overly sensitive.
- Kill those feelings of revenge.
- Mean what you say.

Sometimes it is really hard to lose the revenge syndrome. There is something in us that makes us want to get even. Whether you believe you can get rid of those grudges or not, remember that grudges force you to relive the bad situation over and over again. Grudges make you think about the hurt you personally experienced or the hurt you inflicted upon someone else. You keep reliving a part of your life that you should have dismissed through forgiveness.

Speaking from experience when I've been personally hurt, if I held on to a grudge, I could not have moved forward in my life. I would have been like one of those sisters who just sits back and waits for the right time to snarl at someone or to challenge a person during a public meeting. It is these times when you must "Let Go and Let God." Remember to pray and to ask the Almighty to help you. God is always listening.

VISUALIZATION OR GUIDED CREATIVE IMAGERY

If you have ever daydreamed, or closed your eyes and imagined that you were sitting on the beach in the Bahamas, you are able to draw on the techniques of guided imagery to relieve stress. There are some reports that the "benefits of imagery can be far reaching: by enabling us to communicate with the deep psyche, it reduces stress levels, strengthens our immune defenses, hastens recovery from illness and promotes personal happiness" (Wildwood 1997, p. 142).

Visualization starts with relaxation, followed by bringing forth some pleasant mental image. There are a few steps you can take to prepare yourself. For example, "in one simple exercise known as palming, you close your eyes, cover them with your palms, and concentrate on the color black. Try to make the color fill your whole visual field, screening out any distracting images. To reduce stress, try concentrating first on a color you associate with tension and then mentally replace it with one that you find soothing, red changing to blue" (Guinness 1993, p. 118).

Some reports cite the benefits of visualization with cancer patients. Patients visualize the cancer cells floating in their blood and the white blood cells are shaped like Pac Man, coming along and swallowing them up (Spiegel 1988, p. 63). In another study, Carl and Stephanie Simonton of the Cancer Counseling and Research Center in Fort Worth, Texas, reported on the case of a sixty-one-year-old man who had been advised to practice an imaging exercise several times a day, not just to overcome cancer, but also to rid himself of arthritis and impotence, both of which had plagued him for more than twenty years (Wildwood 1997, p. 143). Also, if you have some pent-up anger, perhaps because of something a meddling sister-in-law did to offend you, blow up a big red balloon and imagine all your anger flowing into it. Once it's full, let it float away, as your troubles and anger flow away.

In another controversial study conducted at Yale University, guided imagery was used on patients who were suffering from severe depression. These patients visualized "scenes in which they were praised by people they admired, a clear boost to their self-esteem" (Wildwood 1997, p. 119).

I have used the terms *guided imagery* and *visualization* interchangeably. Some people separate these concepts because with imagery not only can you conjure up a vision of something, but you can also smell or taste whatever you have conjured up. I will leave it up to you to investigate this technique. However, there are trained therapists to help you learn how to practice this stress buster, and you should locate one of them if you choose to delve more deeply into this technique.

WHAT'S IN A COLOR? COLOR THERAPY

According to color therapy, certain colors can influence your mind and thus your behaviors. "Using a variety of techniques, from color to breathing exercises (whereby the recipient is asked to visualize a specific color as they breathe in and out), to sophisticated light treatment (chromotherapy), they aim to reduce stress levels, and even treat illnesses" (Wildwood 1997, p. 58). Have you noticed that 99 percent of the time the walls of hospitals and mental institutions are painted off-white or eggshell? That's because the pure colors of beige and white make people think of sanitation and cleanliness. One case in 2000 involving an Alabama prison guard put color therapy on center stage. If you missed the hullabaloo, the Alabama jailer painted the men's cells in his jail pink (associated with femininity, babies, and females) as a form of punishment (conveying a subliminal message that jail was for sissies) and as a deterrent to returning to jail. The jailer was basically attempting to use color to reshape the psychological outlook of the prisoners.

Several years ago it was all the rage to have a personal color analysis done to find out which colors were most attractive on you—those that made you look brighter, more alive, and those that flattered your own coloring. Yes, I had my color analysis done and I still follow my color chart. Wearing certain colors definitely gives you a lift. Black and brown are more subdued colors and most often are associated with funerals and conservatives. Unfortunately, some schools and military units require students and recruits to wear uniforms in dark colors like green, navy blue, and gray. By no means are these cheerful or uplifting colors and when you need to boost your psychological outlook, please try to avoid dark, drab colors. Certain shades of yellow are associated with nervous tension and insomnia; green helps to allay anxiety and give a sense of peace and well-being; blue is inspirational and relaxing, and aids in restful sleep; purple enhances spiritual pursuits, such as prayer and meditation; violet and lavender help relieve insomnia; and red boosts vitality (Wildwood 1997, pp. 59–60). Because colors have specific properties, don't paint your bedroom red. It will keep you from falling into a peaceful sleep. Also, be aware of the effect of color when you paint your children's room: determine what color will work best for the effect you want to achieve. As we turn to our next stress buster, remember that your body can stretch you into good health.

YOGA

Yoga originated in India some five thousand years ago and is one of the ancient forms of mind and body relaxation exercise. When I began to sift through stress-busting techniques, yoga was not at the top of my stress-buster list. However, there are some benefits from the techniques used in these body relaxation/stretch exercises that I believe can soothe the daily stress we encounter. Beginners should join an organized class with a seasoned yoga instructor to prevent injury and to gain encouragement. A yoga teacher can also help you incorporate some of the other relaxation techniques (e.g., breathing and visualization) into your yoga practice. As you twist your body into the various positions, you will increase your muscle flexibility and promote blood flow. Other benefits include reducing high blood pressure, pulse rate, and joint pain; increasing your range of motion and your vitality; greater emotional stability; as well as improved concentration, better muscle tone, better posture, and weight loss (Guinness 1993, pp. 220–221). The benefits are there for the taking; however, you must start slowly. That old adage, "No pain, no gain," does not apply to yoga exercise. Yoga is not meant to hurt. Rather, it is meant to take your tired mind and body and put them into a relaxed state. The following are just a few of the many advantages of practicing yoga:

- Can be done anytime
- Can be done anywhere
- Can be done without any special equipment

All that is needed are a few inexpensive items:

- Blanket/mat
- Loose clothing
- Bare feet and/or socks
- Warm room

Once you master the skill of yoga, you can incorporate aromatherapy (e.g., vanilla, fragrances such as bergamot, rose, orange geranium, and primrose) and soft relaxation music into your practice.

African American yoga instructor Maya Breuer of Providence, Rhode Island, offers weekend yoga retreats for women of color. Maya has been a yoga instructor for over ten years and first became involved with yoga at the age of thirty when she was diagnosed with a rare form of gynecological cancer. At the time of her own bout with cancer, Maya was taking care of her terminally ill mother, who subsequently passed away (Hoskins 2000, p. 28). As you can see, Maya was under a tremendous amount of stress, and yoga certainly can be credited with helping her survive these personal crises. Today, at the age of fifty-three, Maya reported to me that she is working with women who bring a variety of life stressors to the yoga sessions. She has found that yoga has helped her physically and psychologically by helping her to "develop goals that she has stuck to." Maya also states that "Yoga has a very high element of behavioral modification that comes from the repetitiveness of the practice." She also notes the importance of taking care of yourself. As such, she watches what she eats, has eliminated sugar and flour from her diet, and rests frequently.

She offers another session that is a real stress buster: Women, Spirit, Moon Meditation. African American women and other women come together once a month for a two-hour session in which they sit in a circle, sing, rock to inspirational music, and dance. The room is filled with various aromatherapeutic candles that help to relieve participants' pent-up stress. Maya reports that these women would come more often, but she is very busy with her training of yoga instructors and working on preparing her manuscript for her first book. Other sessions offered by Maya include yoga set to jazz and drum music, writing workshops, and the importance of high-energy meals and massages.

Select from a list of possible lifesaving stress busters (on page 101) those you feel can help you reduce unwanted stress. Always research your technique thoroughly before you start to practice. Enjoy a less stressful life.

CHAPTER 8

Soothing the Senses

SPAS

The Greek doctor Hippocrates recognized the benefits of natural spring water. The Romans took the use of water seriously and built large structures to house their baths, while the Japanese built geisha houses to take their baths. Africans connected with nature by utilizing water in tribal rituals. The spa movement of the 1800s and early 1900s appeared to taper off for some time, but with the invention of the whirlpool and the fitness center explosion from coast to coast, today you can find opportunities to attend a spa for a day, a weekend, or a month. However, as popular as they have grown over the last twenty years, only 7 percent of the population attending spas are African Americans (Caster 2000, p. 68). As more African American women see the benefits of turning off cell phones and pagers, and sending the kids to their mother-in-law or to a camp, I expect this dismal 7 percent to rapidly increase. In fact, many African American women entrepreneurs are adding spa benefits to their beauty shops.

Spas offer many stress busters, including massages, facials, waxing, a PMS soak for relief, a detoxifying bath in a hydro-tub, massages such as a sea-salt body scrub (my favorite), special skin care treatments for black skin with hyperpigmentation and overactive oil glands, pedicures, manicures, hair coloring, hair styling, meal and diet planning low in fat and high in nutrients, and workshops on topics of particular interest to African American females. These spas, and the African American women who own them, provide a unique service. African American women who were former beauty queens and other professionals own some of the most fabulous spas. On the East Coast, a former beauty queen, Phyllis

McLin, in her New Jersey Clique Salon and Spa offers LaStone therapy, a massage using a hot lava rock, while at the Long Island (New York) Gazelle Day Spa, hot seaweed mud with paraffin wax helps to reduce cellulite. On the West Coast, we find in Pasadena a former Motown executive and now a spa entrepreneur, Toni Patillo, who uses electrotherapy, which claims to tone, slim, strengthen, and heal the body. At In the Mood Spa in Dallas, meanwhile, the former host of ABC's *Home* show, Paula McClure, provides a PMS soak and the Texas Buff and Polish, a body scrub with pecans.

When you decide that you want to pamper yourself, you can choose from a number of soul-satisfying spa treatments. One organization (the Buffalo chapter of Jack and Jill of America) hosted a spa day that I participated in as a Mother's Day activity. Liz Adams, the organizer of this Mother's Day treat, requested that each husband pay for his wife to visit a day spa. The mothers spent a full day relaxing, while the husbands cared for the children. What a wonderful Mother's Day gift!

To ensure that you don't stress yourself out before you go to the spa, you should

- Make your appointment at least three to four weeks in advance. However, there is nothing wrong with making a last-minute appointment. Maybe you just need to get away.
- Leave home in plenty of time to avoid traffic problems and to avoid getting stressed out before your visit.
- Specify whether you want a male or a female therapist when you make your reservation (but check out the literature prior to booking—some spas have only female therapists).
- Think about your modesty level before you book an appointment. Some spas have disposable underpants.
- Be sure to cancel your spa reservation at least twenty-four hours in advance if you need to cancel. Some spas will charge your credit card for last-minute no-shows.
- Remember it is okay to tip.
- Make sure that you clear the spa treatment with your doctor if you have any health conditions. (Women with certain health conditions, such as heart problems, asthma, and diabetes, may experience some reactions as a result of exposure to too much heat or too much cold. Be sure to check.)

One day a month at a spa will work wonders for those stressful days.

Floating Stress Away: Watsu

Watsu, developed by Harold Dull at Harbin Spas in California, is a new and emerging form of water relaxation. This is a form of water exercise whereby a therapist supports and stretches your muscles while you float. In her article "Wondrous Watsu Water Therapy for Mind, Body and Spirit," Judith Lazarus (1999, p. 67) states that "this water therapy is the hottest trend in spa treatment, and not just because it takes place in warm water, ideally 94°C and chest high. The combination of physically therapeutic, relaxing, and meditative aspects of this water massage often transport those who experience it into another plane." As this new spa treatment continues to gain adherents, I expect that African American women will be among those reaping the benefits.

HAND OVER THE RELIEF: MASSAGE

One of the ancient Roman therapies was the massage. Remember the last time you stubbed your toe? The first thing you wanted to do was to start rubbing. Rubbing and the soft touch of someone's hand tend to relieve those tired muscles and bring about a sense of relief and relaxation. If you are a mother, remember when you rubbed your baby's back and he or she fell fast asleep? Massage therapy can have the same effect on you. It has been reported that "preliminary research has shown that massage can temporarily relieve tremors caused by Parkinson's disease, and may work against high blood pressure and reduce agitation in Alzheimer's patients [and] massage increases the level of healthy hormones like serotonin, which helps the body cope with pain and boosts mood" (*Prevention's Healing in Motion* 1999, p. 246).

When you combine a massage with essential oils like sweet almond or sunflower seed, this can greatly enhance your mood. Another prescription for easing muscle pain is a rosemary and olive oil rub. A massage therapist with good hands can locate tight muscles and work to smooth them out, relieving tension and easing out impurities that have built up in the muscles. The benefits you can expect from a good massage are many: massages enhance circulation, alleviate pain and stiffness in muscles and joints, relax you and help to reduce blood pressure, promote sleep, and release the "feel good" hormones. If you add aromatic candles and some soothing music, within a few minutes your stress will begin to dissipate. Of course, you can give yourself a massage, and we do when we apply lotion after a bath or when we rub our aching shoulders. However, I prefer to have a massage therapist loosen those tired shoulder muscles. Don't forget a foot massage with a pedicure and a hand massage with a manicure. Both of these techniques will enhance your mood. They're real stress busters.

AROMATHERAPY

One of the five senses reported to be ten thousand times more sensitive than the other senses, and critical in determining your mood, is the sense of smell (Guinness 1993, p. 328). For example, in the hospital you can go from the nursery where the sweet smell of baby powder makes you feel happy, to another section of the hospital where an unpleasant smell (urine) can change your mood with one whiff. The powerful olfactory nerve is part of the limbic system, which affects our emotions, memory, and certain other mental processes. The olfactory nerve also connects to the hypothalamus, which stimulates the hormones and the all-important master gland, the pituitary. Long recognized in European countries for their beneficial effects on health, aromatic oils are sold in French pharmacies, and insurance plans in some European countries cover prescription costs for them. In recent years African Americans have begun to experience the benefits of essential oils. These oils, taken from plants and flowers, were originally categorized in the nineteenth century by Dr. Edward Bach, who broke away from the traditional medical model and subsequently identified thirty-eight plants with healing properties (Guinness 1993; Wildwood 1997). As Dr. Bach discovered, when we smell something with a pleasant aroma, it can have far-reaching effects on our mind and body's responses.

Make sure you become familiar with any oils that you use because they can evoke both physiological and psychological responses. For example, while a few drops of cinnamon oil may help to clear up congested nasal passages (physiological response), the smell of vanilla, when infused into a hospital treatment room may reduce anxiety in patients facing medical treatment (psychological response). The following section describes some of the olfactory stimulants that can relieve your stress.

Aromatic Smells That Work

I have selected a few of the aromas that I feel can reduce stress. But remember: I caution you to use your judgment and good old common sense before trying some of these suggested aromas. Read other information and delve into the research on your own. It has been reported that certain smells can help remedy certain problematic conditions. Some aromas can help you relax; others may be aphrodisiacs; still others may work as antidepressants. The following scents are reported in the literature to work.

Relaxing smells cedarwood, chamomile, sandalwood, myrrh, mandarin, hops, cypress, juniper berry, sage
Aphrodisiacs cloves, nutmeg, ginger, rose oil, cinnamon, rosemary, jasmine
Antidepressants basil, celery, sage, geranium, lavender, lemon, lime, orange

Now that you have a general overview of some aromas that work, it's time to try them.

Aromatic Bathing: A Stress Buster

An aromatic bath with oils that carry a wonderful relaxing scent can relieve those aching muscles and wash stress down the drain. When you are preparing an aromatic bath, you should "establish which oil (or blend) would best suit your needs, sprinkle four to eight drops [I use eucalyptus oil for tired muscles and a stuffy nose] on the water's surface after the bath has been drawn. Agitate the water to disperse the oil. If you add the essential oil while the water is running, much of the aromatic vapor will evaporate before you enter the bath" (Guinness 1993, p. 328). Because the skin is the largest organ, it absorbs oils fairly quickly, so for those arthritis sufferers who feel pain after a long walk, a few drops of juniper oil added to the bath may help those joints and muscles.

RELAXING HERBS, VITAMINS, JUICES, AND PLANTS

When African slaves were brought to America, they brought their healing knowledge. When the slaves were ill, they were not allowed to call the master's doctor, so they had to rely on alternative treatments from plants and roots they found on the plantations. Now referred to as home remedies, or, in past years, as old wives' treatments, these were cures derived from roots and plants that were used to treat certain ailments. Actually "plants were the only form of medicine until the early twentieth century when manmade drugs came into use . . . and today 25 percent of modern drugs come from botanicals" (Kovach 2002, p. 4). I can remember as a child some unconventional home remedies that my mother and my aunts used. For example, my aunt could not use underarm deodorant because it would cause her to develop boils, so she used baking soda instead. Today we find baking soda in toothpaste, deodorant, and a host of other personal-hygiene products. Herbs are now widely recognized for their curative powers. However, in America, because of the many federal regulations governing the approval and distribution of medicinal drugs and the rules covering insurance company reimbursement of some alternative treatments, research is still needed to provide solid evidence to the government and the public about the value of these products. In this regard we, as African American women, must follow the practices that have been approved; however, we should also explore other approaches to managing our stress. For example, African American women have a very high incidence of heart disease; therefore, it is wise to consider taking an herb like "garlic powder [which] helps to prevent heart disease because it can lower total cholesterol and triglycerides, and boosts levels of 'good' HDL cholesterol while lowering 'bad' LDL cholesterol. Garlic also can kill a number of germs, including bacteria, viruses and fungi" (O'Brien 1998, p. 9). Remember: you must tell your medical provider if you're using any alternate treatments. Also it has been reported that eating fish once a week

can lower the risk of heart disease by 30 percent. This study followed 85,000 women for fourteen years before reporting on these results. Further, fish like salmon, tuna, herring, and mackerel, which are high in omega-3 fatty acids, may lower cholesterol and increase blood clotting (Brophy 2002).

Herbs are simply an option and by no means am I suggesting their use as a replacement for your doctor's treatment plan. However, I am over fifty years of age and have used garlic on my chicken, pizza, and spaghetti for most of my life, and my blood pressure is low—below 110/60. The choice is up to you and your physician. O'Brien (1998) also reports that ginger root dissolves blood clots while echinacea, astragalus, and ginseng can strengthen the immune system. You must treat herbs with respect, however, because they may have side effects, such as the effect of kava kava on motor reflexes and judgment (Kovach 2002, p. 48). So, again, always let your physician know what you are taking.

Allergies affect over 40 million people, including a vast number of African Americans. When a foreign agent attacks the immune system, it sparks an allergic reaction. The immune system responds by pouring antihistamines into our bloodstream to fight these allergens. Symptoms may include swollen, itchy eyes and a runny nose. O'Brien reports that the herb eyebright will relieve itchy eyes, nettle herb will relieve a runny nose (do not take this herb if you have high blood pressure), and reishi mushroom has a strong antihistamine action. Information on additional herbal remedies and other items that are reportedly effective in addressing certain stress disorders/illnesses is included in the Stress Buster chart.

Stress Buster Chart

The information provided in Table 8.1 is offered for reference only and is not meant to replace any medical advice you have received from your health care provider. It is a compilation of what others have written on various approaches to managing stress.

FOODS THAT WIND US UP AND HERBS THAT CALM US DOWN

Foods affect us in a variety of ways: some wind us up; others have a calming effect. It was reported that "turkey, chicken and nuts contain tryptophan, [which] boosts serotonin and helps ward off stress-related symptoms" and cooked spinach, whole-wheat bread, and fortified cereals contain magnesium, which helps balance serotonin levels and prevent headaches (*First for Women* 1998, p. 43). Foods that should be avoided if you want to reduce stress are sugar, caffeine, and alcohol. Also, to unwind, try juices made from fennel or lettuce as they have a sedative effect

Stress Busters Chart*

Stressrelated Illnesses or Illnesses That May Be Affected By Stress	Techniques	Teas and Other Remedies	Other Reported Possible Remedies
Diabetes		Herb: bitter melon lowers blood pressure	To reduce blood sugar: celery seeds and garlic
Constipation	Walking/exercise		Herbs: basil; Foods: asparagus,spinach, carrots, apples, olive oil, alfalfa
Acne		Tea: roobioos	Selenium (antioxidant); basil, zinc,tea tree oil, Vitamins: A,B6,E,water
Anxiety	Warm bath with a few drops of balm or lavender added to bath water	Teas: chamomile, primrose, catnip	Meditation, prayer.reduce your intake of caffeine; Aroma Therapy: vanilla scented candles; Herbs passionflower, valerian
Backache	Mustard patch	Teas: chamomile ,burdock	Meditation and relaxation; Herb: garlic
Flu/Cold	Rest and read a good inspirational book or Bible	Teas: echinacea, ginger, peppermint, elderberry, ginseng, boneset, licorice, black walnut, rose hip	Juice: Orange Juice. Other: eucalyptus oil a few drops in warm water inhaled to clear sinuses
Headache	Biofeedback	Teas: fever few, lavender, marjoram, peppermint, ginger, sage	Meditation, Relaxation, evening primrose oil, Warm Bath: add a few drops of Rosemary oil and Eucalyptus oil
Insomnia	Biofeedback	Teas: skullcap, lemon Balm, peppermint, valerian, chamomile, motherwart	Meditation and relaxation or Combine 2oz almond oil, 10 drops each bergamot and petitgraim oils, 3 drops rose geranium essential and, 1#-drop neroli essential oil into a tubful of warm water and soak. Herb: passionflower
Sore Throat		Teas: blueberries, ginger root, goldenseal, licorice	Food: pineapple

(continued)

Table 8.1. (continued)

Urinary Track		Teas: cranberries, raspberries, blackberries, Herb:uva ursi	Foods: watermelon, strawberries and water
Stroke	Biofeedback, meditation walking		Herbs: garlic and evening primrose oil
Hypertension	Biofeedback,massage	Tea; damiana	Herb: fo-ti, hawthorn
Cancer		Tea: green tea	Foods: brussels sprouts, cabbage, broccoli, cauliflower, kale, turnips, carrots, kohlrabi
Heart Disease		Herb:hawthorn	lecithin,ginkgo biloba, fo-ti (Chinese herb reduces blood pressure)hawthorne, onions
Ulcers	Relaxation and Meditation		marigold
Depression		Teas: St John's wart, ginseng and sage	Herb: lemon balm
Migraine Headache	Biofeedback	Tea: rosemary	Herb: thyme,feverfew
Panic Attack			Tea: fennel
Menopause Stress Symptoms		Teas: anise, fenugreek, red clover	Herb: anise foods: soy bean products, dong quai, ginger,sage, St John's wart
Cystitis			Nutrients: cranberries, strawberries,raspberries, blackberries, watermelon
PMS	Aerobic exercise	Teas:dong quai, buchu, raspberry, dandelion	Foods: tomato, cucumber, radish juice, parsley
Yeast infections		cranberry	Yogurt,spinach,turnip greens,water,Herd; garlic

*For the sources of information contained in this table, see the Appendix.

(Justice 2000b, p. 29). In addition, juices made from cantaloupe and nec-tarines are rich in beta-carotene and vitamins to relax and soothe the colon. All soda that contains caffeine should be avoided.

Some herbs are also reported to have helpful properties. For instance, "In studies in Mexico and Sweden, people who took Ginseng for 12 weeks said their quality of life improved more than those who took only a vita-min or placebo. Ginseng also helped increase vigor of one group of 36 people with non–insulin dependent diabetics" (Lehrman 2000, p. 36). Also, the American Indians have "long used [the herb black cohosh] for menopausal symptoms (avoid if taking tamoxifen or treated for cancer) and today in Europe [it is] standard medical treatment for premenstrual syndrome, painful periods and menopausal symptoms, including relief from [hot] flashes. It's gaining use in the U.S. as well, because medical studies have shown that this herb can be as effective as hormone replace-ment without the side effects" (Kovach 2002, p. 21).

The new bottled waters with natural additives or herbal drinks also may help to boost your energy level. In addition, the so-called power bars sold in health food stores and health clubs may alter your mood by giving you that power boost. However, it is important to read the nutrition labels on these products because their claims may not be substantiated (Golden 2002, p. 96). These are but a few of the foods and juices that may help you take control of stress.

CHAPTER 9

The Afrocentric Network: Family, Work, Community, and Social Support

Women begin to develop their social support network during their adolescent years. They draw on relationships from individuals they interact with. These people make up the African American woman's Afrocentric network. Others who are not within the Afrocentric circle still provide some social support, so they will be mentioned for information purposes.

African American women receive most of their social support at home, at work, and in the community through both formal and informal channels. From our formal social support network, we may receive financial support and counseling, while our informal social network gives us emotional support or recognition for our community service. For this discussion, I focus on the informal social support we receive from relationships in our family, at work, and in the community and our membership in various organizations, emphasizing why these relationships are important to our well-being.

SOCIAL SUPPORT, HEALTH STATUS, AND LONGEVITY: WHY WE NEED OUR FAMILY

There has always been a very strong social network operating in the African American community and among family members. In Africa, we maintained a strong sense of family and community. This strong family ethic survived under the ills of slavery and continued in America as a strong, new, Underground Railroad network of family was built. It is the African American women's family and extended family in the community that provide her with the support needed to survive the daily assault of stress. According to Keith (1997, p. 100), "A considerable body of research has established that persons who are enmeshed in strong family and friendships networks are less likely to succumb to the damaging effects of stress and, therefore, are more likely to enjoy higher levels of mental health." As presented in part I, African American women's health status and longevity statistics are poor. With the extensive empirical research findings showing the positive impact that family social support has on health status, it is clear that we must continue to nurture and strengthen our family ties.

WORK, COLLEAGUES, AND SOCIAL SUPPORT IN THE WORKPLACE

African American women spend a tremendous amount of their day at work. During these hours, they have many engaging conversations and interactions with colleagues. It is during these conversations and interactions that the African American female employee may encounter stressors. Therefore, African American women must find buffers that will help shield them from the negative effects of work-related stressors. One buffer that can be enlisted to assist with the stressors is other African American women or a coworker who can lend social support. Social support in the workplace can help the African American woman deal more effectively with some of the attacks she receives from a variety of occupational stressors like racism, sexism, oversupervision, low expectation of her ability, excessive work demands, and jealousy, to mention just a few.

Social support is rendered by colleagues who support you or who are your supporters. A colleague whose opinion you value can be very useful during work hours to discuss a problem, make suggestions, or just be there if you should need assistance or a shoulder to lean on (or to cry on, in some instances). However, if you cry at work, you should seriously consider leaving that job or that profession.

One of the problems faced by African American women in the workplace, especially in academia and in corporate America, is the paucity of other African American women who can lend their support when needed. This is exacerbated by a job market in which it's "last hired, first fired." Despite this obstacle to advancement, many African American women are slowly moving into corporate positions that have historically been closed to them. In academia, on the other hand, tenure is the sorting and controlling factor for African American women's survival, as we continue to experience a dwindling of minority faculty each year. This is a setting in which an African American woman may be the only person of color on her professional level, isolating her from the support of other African American women when a crisis arises. Yes, other majority women could be a real asset to her; however, as mentioned previously, some white majority women may lend their support to white men in the workplace rather than minority women.

If the major stressor is a majority female and there are no other supporters, an African American woman in the workplace will have a very high occupational stress level because she is alone. In this case, she needs informational support. This is the type of social support a person needs because "it provides the person with information that the person can use in coping with personal and environmental issues" (House 1981, p. 25). When an African American woman receives this kind of feedback and support, which amounts to a stress buffer, the effects of the stressor may have far less of an impact on the person's health. It is extremely important for an African American woman to have close friends and colleagues in the workplace. She must sit on and, yes, volunteer for a position on search committees. For only through her participation in the process and identification of prospective candidates of color can she eliminate the loneliness she may be experiencing. Having an African American woman support your ideas during a faculty/staff meeting or sharing information about the workplace with you will help to make the workplace a little more tolerable and will take less of a toll on your health behavior (excessive smoking and eating are reactions to stress). By no means is it guaranteed that other African American women colleagues will be your workplace supporters (as mentioned in chapter 4); however, if we as African American women do not support each other, how can we ever expect to make a difference as a people?

COMMUNITY, FRIENDS, AND SOCIAL SUPPORT

African Americans have always had to rely on a network of individuals within their immediate community to provide social support for their needs. The majority community provided no assistance for newly freed slaves and later Jim Crow laws prevented African Americans from sharing in the American Dream afforded to so many European transplants. Out of necessity, African Americans were forced to create a form of mutual aid for their community through an Afrocentric Underground Railroad model. This form of social support was not foreign to the African slaves who brought with them community-oriented tribal traditions and replicated in America this strong community network (in West Africa, thousands of African slaves had a strong kinship/community/social support network). However, American history has omitted or inaccurately reported certain aspects of African American history. For example, following the Civil War, the first black schools and welfare institutions were founded not by white missionaries, as Americans are led to believe, but by "black men and women who pooled their pennies, organized fish fries and church suppers, and took care of themselves" (Bennette 2001, p. 88).

As Bennette notes in his article, "10 Biggest Lies about Black History," Americans have been led to believe that African Americans wanted someone else to take care of their needs other than themselves. He points out that "by 1831 there were more than 43 Black benevolent or mutual aid societies in Philadelphia alone and you found very few blacks in an Almshouse" (p. 94). Founded and operated by African American communities, there were mutual aid societies formed by 1780, women's clubs by 1889, and rent parties in the 1930s, all providing social support in African American communities. In fact, "this tradition of self help and communal support spilled over into the twentieth century with the work of Black women's clubs, Black ministers, and fraternal organizations" (Bennette 2001, p. 94).

Social support through African American women's organizations, clubs, and sororities continues to be one of the greatest strengths of the African American community. It is through membership in these organizations that the African American community receives millions of dollars in financial support. African American women join these organizations for a variety of reasons, not only to help their community but also because, through their membership, they are provided with personal support. According to Myers (1991, p. 14), "As Black women, we affirm one another's sense of self-worth through open dialogue about our common experiences. Emotional strength can be gained by sharing common life experiences [and it has also been] found that an influence on African American women's coping with oppression was the feedback offered by those whose opinions mattered to them, that is, other African American women." When these women meet to discuss issues that are related to their community, they are able to unload some of the stress they have accumulated from unpleasant interaction with others (e.g., at work). Many African American women make lifelong friends through membership in certain organizations (e.g., Masonic, family, or Greek organizations): Through my membership in Jack and Jill of America, Inc. and The Links, I have found friendships with Diane Turner of New Haven, Connecticut and Barbara Martin of Westchester County, New York, through "For Women Only," friendship with Barbara Penn of Chicago and through Daughters of Isis, Patricia Moore of New Jersey.

Each of these social support systems can serve as a place to deposit your stress or can become a source of stress. African American women join organizations for a variety of reasons, such as a need for friendship, to help their community by raising funds, or just to be part of something worthwhile. But to avoid stress, always read the goals and objectives of the organization before you join. For example, if you want to build homes for migrant farmers, but the organization's goal is to provide education programs for the children of migrant farmers, when the membership meets to discuss its stated purpose and that purpose does not meet your needs, you will be caused more stress.

Unfortunately, some friends can be a source of tremendous stress. In her article "When Friends Create Stress," Janet Bailey (2001, p. 44) states, "Think twice before you go to your friends for stress relief." She further cites research from Ohio State University in which forty women were asked to confront a store manager about a defective purchase. These women, who brought a friend along, had a greater increase in cholesterol (a response to stress) than those without a friend present. Sometimes having our friends with us during certain critical situations may cause us to worry that they may think poorly of us. As mentioned previously, African American women do hold the opinions of others to be very important. However, only you can be the judge of how much you want to confide in a friend. I find that I rely on some of my friends more than others. In addition, I am very guarded as to how much I want to burden my friends with. That's why other stress busters like prayer and meditation can be another way to help you *lay your burdens down.*

CONCLUSIONS

The events of September 11, 2001, and the war with Iraq, have added another stressor to the long list of stressors that African American women must deal with on a daily basis. As I mentioned in part I of this book, there are some stressors that we have no control over, and the tragedy in New York City and Washington, D.C., fits into this category. However, we cannot simply block out the media that constantly reminds Americans that we are vulnerable to outside forces, and we cannot block out reports of racial profiling and overpolicing of African American communities. However, with all the faults in America, we African American women love our country. And it is because of this love that we must keep our stress levels under control so that we can help our families, our friends, and this great nation. It is my hope that when you have read this book, you will discuss your feelings with individuals who can lend their social support, and you will incorporate and practice one or more of the de-stressors found in this book. You will find that they can help. Some are simply common sense; others are amusing; and still others are serious and should be given serious consideration before you engage in them. In addition, you will find a "Stress Reduction Contract for Life" (SRCL) in Table 9.1. To complete the contract, fill it out as indicated in each column. This SRCL is one tool for you to use. As you begin to identify your stressors, you may also uncover a pattern that must be controlled. In order to live a long and healthy and less stressful life, it takes effort and determination. We, as African American women, have survived for more than four hundred years. This hasn't

Table 9.1
Stress Reduction Contract for Life

IDENTIFIED STRESSOR (Include all the stressors that are impacting your life)	DATE, TIME, PLACE (Identify the location, work, home, club, etc.	YOUR REACTION List how you felt, physically, when the stress occurred	BEHAVIOR EXHIBITED List behaviors you notice; smoking more, eating more, etc.	SOLUTION The most important column. Here you decide what you will do to combat or buffer yourself from the effects of the stress you are encountering. Write down how you plan to handle the stress.

been easy, and some African Americans have succumbed to the stresses of life at a young age (Phyllis Himan, Jennifer Holiday, Donnie Hathway, Billy Holiday). I have identified the who, why, what, and where of stress and offered many solutions, but, ultimately, it's up to you to take control of your life.

I wish you longevity and healthy living. God Bless.

Epilog: A Victim of September 11

JANICE MARIE SCOTT

Janice Marie Scott was born on October 12, 1954, in Memphis, Tennessee. In 1955, her mother moved the family to Milwaukee, Wisconsin, where Janice attended the local public school until her early teen years. Janice then moved with her family in the early 1970s to Colorado Springs, Colorado. There, she graduated from Harrison High School on May 28, 1972. Demonstrating a selfless commitment to her family, shortly after graduation she took on the task of caring for her youngest sister, Darlene, as well as her niece Gail, daughter of Janice's oldest sister, Claudette, while Claudette took an overseas assignment in Germany.

In 1975, Janice met Abraham Scott, a native of Beaufort, South Carolina, who was assigned as a second lieutenant to the 4th Finance Company at Fort Carson near Colorado Springs. Janice and Abraham were married in Beaufort, on December 27, 1976. Two years later, the couple was blessed with their first child, Crystal.

In December 1978, the family moved to Fort Benjamin Harrison in Indiana where Janice began to embark upon a career in finance, which began with the Indiana National Bank in downtown Indianapolis. Janice and Crystal then moved with Abraham to Fort Rucker, Alabama, in July 1979. Her career was temporarily placed on hold; however, she continued her education at Enterprise (Alabama) State Junior College, where she received an associate's degree in business administration.

In August 1982, the family moved to Heidelberg, Germany, where Janice took courses at the Heidelberg campus of the University of Maryland.

She also continued her career with the local credit union and then entered the U.S. federal government workforce as a check control officer with the Army Finance Office in Switzingen, Germany. Following this position, she was hired as an accountant with the European Army Accounting Office in Leiman, Germany.

During the mid-1980s, the family moved just outside Washington, D.C., where in 1986, Angel entered their lives. It did not take Janice long to re-enter the government workforce. The Army Personnel Command in Alexandria, Virginia, hired her in 1987 as an assistant budget officer. She also continued to further her education by taking night and weekend classes at the University of Maryland in College Park. She graduated on December 23, 1988, with a bachelor of science degree in business administration. This great achievement was instrumental in helping her to land a bud-get analyst position in 1989 with Resource Services Washington in the Office of the Administrative Assistant to the Secretary of the Army in the Pentagon. Janice was promoted in June 2001 as a supervisory budget analyst–team leader with Resource Services Washington. She was employed by this organization when terrorists flew a plane into the Pentagon on September 11, 2001. She was only a few credits shy of becoming a Certified Government Financial Manager, the government equivalent of a Certified Public Accountant.

Janice's commitment to children, her community, and her personal growth led to her involvement in a number of organizations. She was a member of Blacks in Government, the 5-Star Toastmasters Club, the Association of Government Accountants, and the Greater Little Zion Baptist Church, in Fairfax, Virginia. In 1992 Janice became a member of the Burke-Fairfax (VA) Chapter of Jack and Jill of America, Incorporated. She held several offices with the Burke-Fairfax Chapter: 1993–1995 Historian, 1995–1997 Program Director, 1997–1999 Vice President, 1999–2001 Program Director, and was the current Foundation Chair 2001–2003. In addition to her participation on the Executive Board, Janice chaired various chapter committees: Community Service, Black History Forum, Health Initiative, Program, By-Laws, and Foundation & Legislation. As a result of her hard work with the Burke-Fairfax Chapter, she was honored as Distinguished Mother and was nominated again for a second year.

Janice is survived by her mother, Geraldine Holmes; her husband, Abraham Scott; her daughters, Crystal and Angel M. Scott; her sisters, Claudette Staley, Delores James, Denise Holmes, Willette Wages, and Darlene Caldwell; her brother, George Holmes; and a host of nieces, nephews, and other relatives.

In Your Memory I Honor Your Contribution to the African American Community.

Appendix

Afrika, Llaila. 1998. *African Holistic Health.* New York: A&B Publishers Group.

Balch, James A., and Phyllis Balch. 1997. *Prescription for Nutritional Healing.* New York: Penguin.

Brophy, Christine. 2002. "Fish Fight Heart Disease." *Family Circle,* 8 August, p. 86.

Castleman, Micheal. 2001. "10 Ways to Boost Your Immune Power." *Family Circle,* June 2, pp. 87–94.

Dewey, Laurel. 1999. *Heal Your Body Instantly.* Lantana, Fla.: American Media Mini Mags.

———. 2001. *Folk Medicine.* Boca Raton, Fla.: American Media Mini Mags.

Golden, Fredric. 2002. "Power of Foods: Do They Work?" *New York Times Magazine,* 21 January, p. 81.

Grew, John C. 1991. "20 Ways to Reduce Your Cancer Risk." *Essence,* February, pp. 20–22.

Guinness, Alma E., ed. 1993. *Family Guide to Natural Medicine: How to Stay Healthy the Natural Way.* Pleasantville, N.Y.: Readers Digest Association.

Horowitz, Janice. 2002. "10 Foods That Pack a Wallop." *New York Times Magazine,* 21 January, pp. 74–78.

Jibrin, Janis. 2000. "The Super Foods: Surprising Ways to Stay Well." *Women's Day,* 1 September, p. 129.

Justice, L. A. 2000a. *Beat Stress.* Boca Raton, Fla.: American Media Mini Mags.

———. 2000b. *Healing Juices.* Boca Raton, Fla.: American Media Mini Mags.

Kovach, Sue. 2002 *Herbs That Work Better Than Drugs.* Boca Raton, Fla.: American Media Mini Mags.

Long, Delores. 2001. *Nature's Healing Secrets.* Boca Raton, Fla.: American Media Mini Mags.

Long, Patricia. 1992. "Can Foods Heal?" *Glamour,* November, pp. 270–71.

"Nature's Best Medicine: Foods that Fight Disease." 2002. *Family Circle,* 2 March, pp. 71–74.

"99 Herbal Cures for Women." 2001. *Women's Health Special, Prevention Guide,* 26 January, pp. 16–77.

O'Brine, James. 2000. *Herbal Cures for Common Ailments.* Boca Raton, Fla.: America Media Mini Mags.

Parents Magazine, October 2001, p. 67.

Rabkin, Rachel. 2002. "Herbal Remedies That Really Work." *Family Circle,* 11 November, centerfold.

Rohlfing, Carla. 1991. "Anticancer Diet—What to Eat Now." *Family Circle,* 20 May, pp. 94–99.

Stanley, Louise. 2002. *Garlic, Vinegar and Honey.* Boca Raton, Fla.: American Media Mini Mags.

"Top 10 in 1991." 1991. *US News & World Report,* 20 May, pp. 94–99.

Wildwood, C. 1997. *The Complete Guide to Reducing Stress.* London: Judy Piatkus Publishers.

Bibliography

Adams, LaGina. 2001. "More Work and Less Pay." *Black Enterprise*, February, p. 42.

Adler, Eric. 1999. "Study Finds Evidence of Healing Power of Prayer." *Buffalo News*, 31 October, sec. A, p. 8.

Afrika, Llaila. 1998. *African Holistic Health*. New York: A&B Publishers Group.

American Cancer Society. 1998. *Health Fact Sheet*, p. 9.

Bacon, C. L., R. Rennecker, and M. Kuther. 1952. "Psychosomatic Survey of Cancer of the Breast." *Psychosomatic Medicine* 4: pp. 453–60.

Bailes, Frederick. 1971. *Your Mind Can Heal You*. Marina Del Ray, Calif.: DeVorss Publications.

Bailey, Janet. 2001. "When Friends Create Stress." *Redbook,* May, p. 44.

Balch, James A., and Phyllis Balch. 1997. *Prescription for Nutritional Healing*. New York: Penguin.

Ballweg, Rachel. 2000. "7 Simple Ways to Reduce Stress." *Better Homes and Gardens,* January, pp. 62–68.

Barbie, E. L. 1992. "African American Women and Depression: A Review and Critique of the Literature." *Archives of Psychiatric Nursing* 7, no. 5: pp. 257–65.

Beard, Hilary. 2002. "Is Your Job Making You Sick?" *Essence*, March, pp. 64–67.

Bennette, Lerone. 2001. "10 Biggest Lies about Black History." *Ebony*, May, pp. 86–94.

Bernstein, Aaron. 2001. "Racism in the Workplace." *Business Week,* 30 July, pp. 64–68.

Bertram-Brooks, P. 1996. "African American Women: Disfigured Images in Epidemiology of Depression." In *African American Women Health and Social Issues,* ed. Catherine Collins, pp. 107–32. Westport, Conn.: Greenwood Publishing Group.

Black Career Women, http//www.BCW.com; Voting Center results. Accessed October 10, 2001.

Bolden, Tonya. 1999. *Mother Love's "Forgive or Forget: Never Underestimate the Power of Forgiveness."* New York: HarperCollins.

Bonneau, R. 1994. "Experimental Approaches to Identify Mechanism of Stress-Induced Modulation of Immunity to Herpes Simples Virus Infection." In *Handbook of Human Stress and Immunity,* eds. R. Glaser and K. J. Glaser, pp. 125–53. New York: Academic Press.

Booger, C. 1999. *Smart Guide to Relieving Stress.* New York: Cader Company.

Booker, Vonetta. 2001. "Beyond the Banana Seat: Mind Body Fitness." *Essence,* May, p. 88.

Bouchez, Colette. 1994. "Heart Diseases: The Lady Killer." *Daily News,* September 19, p. A10.

Bowser, Benjamin, and Raymond Hunt. 1996. *Impacts of Racism on White Americans,* 2d ed. Thousands Oaks, Calif.: Sage Publications.

"Breathe Away Fat." 1997. *First in Fitness, First for Women,* October 20, p. 22.

Brophy, Christine. 2002. "Fish Fight Heart Disease." *Family Circle,* 8 August, p. 86.

Brown, Monique. 2000. "Medicine or Magic?" *Consumer Life Black Enterprise,* May, p. 165.

Burke, M. A., and K. Goodken. 1997. "Stress and the Development of Breast Cancer: A Persistent and Popular Link Despite Contrary Evidence." *Cancer* 79, no. 5: pp. 1055–59.

"Burnished or Burn Out: The Delights and Dangers of Working in Health." 1994. *The Lancet,* 10 December, pp. 1583–84.

Burton, Linda M. 1992. "Black Grandparents Rearing Children of Drug-Addicted Parents: Stressors, Outcomes and Social Services Needs." *The Gerontologist* 32, no. 6: pp. 744–51.

Campbell, Don. 1997. *The Mozart Effect.* New York: Avon Books.

"Cardinal Principles for Making a Slave." 1970. Black Arcade Liberation Library. http://www.afrocentricnews.com/html/lynch.htm. Accessed April 25, 2003.

Cassileth, B. R. 1996. "Stress and the Development of Breast Cancer: A Persistent and Popular Link Despite Contrary Evidence." *Cancer* 77, no. 6: pp. 1015–1516.

Caster, Marcia Day. 2000. "Dreams a Round of Black-Owned Spas around the Country." *Heart and Soul,* August/September, pp. 68–72.

Castleman, Micheal. 2001. "10 Ways to Boost Your Immune Power." *Family Circle,* 2 June, pp. 87–94.

Charger, N. 1990. "Racial and Gender Discrimination: Risk Factors for High Blood Pressure." *Social Sciences Medical* 30: pp. 1273–81.

Chatters, Linda. 1997. *Family Life in Black America.* Thousand Oaks, Calif.: Sage Publications.

Childre, D. L. 1994. *Freeze Frame.* Boulder Creek, Calif.: Planetary Publications.

Cohen, Harry. 2002. "Power of Prayer." *Today* Show, NBC (November 1).

Cohen, Reese, L. B. Kaplan, and R. E. Reggero. 1986. "Coping with Stress of Arthritis." In *Arthritis and the Elderly,* eds R. W. Moskowitz and M. Houg, pp. 47–56. New York: Springer.

Collins, Catherine. 1990. "A Comparison of the Effects of Elementary School Health Instructional Programs and Parent Child Rearing on the Health Practices of School Children." EDD. diss., State University of New York at Buffalo.

————. 1996. "Commentary on the Health and Social Status of African American Women." In *African American Women's Health and Social Issues,* ed. Catherine Collins, pp. 1–10. Westport, Conn.: Greenwood Publishing Group.

"Combat Job Stress: Does Work Make You Sick?" www.convoke.com/markjr/cstress.html. Accessed October 11, 2001.

Cook, Susan J. 1998. *Too Blessed to Be Stressed.* Nashville: Thomas Nelson Publishers.

Coontz, Stephanie. 1992. *The Way We Never Were.* New York: Basic Books.

Cornish, Grace. 1998. *10 Bad Choices That Ruin Black Women's Lives.* New York: Crown Publishers.

Crawford-Green, C. 1996. "Hypertension and African American Women." In *African American Women's Health and Social Issues,* ed. Catherine Collins, pp. 59–75. Westport Conn.: Greenwood Publishing Group.

Davidson, J. 1999. "Overworked Americans or Overwhelmed Americans." *Vital Speeches* 5, no. 15: p. 470–74.

Davis, Ayana. 2000. "Let It Go." *Heart and Soul,* August/September, p. 86.

Davis, M., E. Eshelman, and M. McKay. 1995. *The Relaxation and Stress Reduction Workbook.* Oakland, Calif.: New Harbinger Publications.

Dawkins, P. Marvin, and C. Graham Kinlock. 2000. *African American Golfers during the Jim Crow Era.* Westport, Conn.: Praeger Publications.

Derrick, Rachel. 1997. "Healing the Wounds of Racism." *Essence,* March, p. 37.

Dewey, Laurel. 1999. *Heal Your Body Instantly.* Lantana, Fla.: American Media Mini Mags.

————. 2001. *Folk Medicine.* Boca Raton, Fla.: American Media Mini Mags.

Dodd, M., and K. Doner. 2002. "The Get Smart Health Guide." *Working Mothers,* February, pp. 50–58.

Duhart, O. 1996. "The Hypertension Threat." In *Health Quest: The Publication of Black Wellness, Black History Special,* pp. 6–8. Levas, Inc.: Chalfont, PA.

Dunnavant, Sylvia. 1995. *Celebrating Life: African American Women Speak Out.* Dallas: USF Inc. Publishers.

Eberlein, T. 1998. "How Stressed Are You? A Personalized Test" *The Redbook Report,* January, pp. 90–93.

Edlin, G., E. Golanty, and K. Brown. 1996. *Health and Wellness,* 5th ed. Boston: Jones and Bartlett Publications.

Edwards, Audrey. 1998. "Black and White: What Still Divides Us?" *Essence,* March, pp. 77–80, 138–140.

Eitzen, D. Stanley, and Maxine Zinn. 1989. *The Shaping of America: Social Consequences of the Changing Economy.* Englewood Cliffs, N.J.: Prentice Hall.

Ezorsky, Gertrude. 1995. *Affirmative Action Promotes Equality in Education and Work, Opposing Viewpoints.* San Diego, Calif.: Greenhaven Press.

Feagin, J., and M. Sikes. 1995. *Living with Racism: The Black Middle Class Experience.* Boston: Beacon Press.

Fisher, S., R. Cooper, L. Weber, and Y. Liao. 1996. "Psychological Correlates of Chest Pain among African American Women." *Women and Health* 24, no. 3: pp. 19–35.

"5 Minute Cure for Stress." 1998. *First for Women,* 6 April, pp. 42–43.

Flewellyn, Valada S. 1990. *Poetically Just Us.* St. Paul, Minn.: Parker Initiatives Publications.

Franklin, Hope John. 1988. "A Historical Note on Black Families." In *Black Families*, 2d ed., ed. Harriette Pipes McAdoo, pp. 20–26. Newbury Park, Calif.: Sage Publishing.

Frazier, E. Franklin. 1966. *The Negro Family in the United States*. Chicago: University of Chicago Press. Original edition, 1939.

Freire, Paulo. 1968. *Pedagogy of the Oppressed*. New York: Herder and Herder.

Friedman, E., A. Katcher, and V. Brightman. 1977. "Incidence of Recurrent Herpes Labialis Upper Respiratory Infections: A Prospective Study of the Influence of Biologic, Social and Psychological Predictors." *Oral Surgery* 43: pp. 873–78.

Gates, David. 1993 "White Male." *Newsweek,* 29 March, pp. 48–53.

Genovese, Eugene. 1991. "The Myth of the Absent Family." In *The Black Family Essay and Studies,* 4th ed., ed. Robert Staples, pp. 5–23. Belmont, Calif.: Wadsworth Publishing.

Gilkes, Cheryl. 1985. "Together and in Harness: Women's Traditions in the Sanctified Church." *Signs Journal for Women* 10, no. 4 (Summer): pp. 678–87.

Girlhome@aol.com. 2001. "Black Golfer Takes a Long Shot, Finds His Spot in History 52 Years Later." Accessed March 20.

Glazer, Nathan. 1975. *Affirmative Discrimination*. New York: Basic Books.

Golden, Fredric. 2002. "Power Foods: Do They Work?" *New York Times Magazine,* 21 January, pp. 82–84, 96–97.

Gorman, Christine. 2002. "Walk Don't Run." *New York Times Magazine,* 21 January, p. 82.

Grant Goldsby, Gwendolyn. 1995. *The Best Kind of Loving: A Black Woman's Guide to Finding Intimacy*. New York: HarperCollins Publishers.

Greene, Katherine, and Richard Greene. 1995. "The 20 Top Paid Women in Corporate America," *Working Women,* 20, no. 1: p. 36.

Greer, Morris S. 1975. "The Psychological Attributes of Women Who Develop Breast Cancer: A Controlled Study." *Journal of Psychosomatic Research* 19: pp. 147–53.

Grew, John C. 1991. "20 Ways to Reduce Your Cancer Risk." *Essence,* February, pp. 20–22.

Grudy, J. J., L. A. Aday, D. Zhang, and R. J. Winn. 1997. "The Role of Informal and Formal Social Support Networks for Patients with Cancer." *Cancer Practice* 5, no. 4 (July/August): pp. 241–46.

Guinness, Alma E., ed. 1993. *Family Guide to Natural Medicine: How to Stay Healthy the Natural Way*. Pleasantville, N.Y.: Readers Digest Association.

Gutman, Herbert. 1975. "Persistent Myths about the African American Family." *Journal of Interdisciplinary History* 6: pp. 181–210.

Hacker, Andrew. 1992. *Two Nations Black and White, Separated, Hostile, Unequal*. New York: Ballantine Books.

Harlow, K., R. Johnson, and P. Callen. 1993. "A Comparison of Physical Health Benefits Utilization: Mental and Physical Health Claimants, 1989 and 1990." *Journal of Occupational Medicine,* 35, no. 3, pp. 275–77.

Hart, Archibald. 1992. *Stress and Your Child: Know the Signs and Prevent the Harm*. Dallas: Word Publishing.

Hartman, Heida I. 1989. "Changes in Women's Economic and Family Roles in Post–World War II United States." In *The Reshaping of America*, eds. D. Stanley

Eitzen and Maxine Beca Zinn, pp. 296–318. Englewood Cliffs, N.J.: Prentice Hall.

Health, United States 2001 With Urban & Rural Health Chartbook. 2001. Hyattsville, Md.: U.S. Department of Health and Human Services, Centers for Disease Control and Prevention, National Center for Health Statistics.

Hill, Anita. 1997 *Speaking Truth to Power.* New York: Dell Publishing Group.

Hirch, C. D., P. Kent, and L. Silverman. 1972. "Homogeneity and Heterogeneity among Low Income Negro and White Aged." In *Research Planning and Action for Elderly: The Power and Potential of Social Science*, ed. D. P. Kent, R. Kastenbaum, and S. Sherwood, pp. 484–500. New York: Behavioral Publications.

Hobfoll, Stevan. 1985. *Stress, Social Support and Women.* Washington D.C.: Hemisphere Publishing Corporation.

Homo-Delarchef, C., F. Fitzpatrick, N. Christeff, and B. A. Bach. 1991. "Six Steroids, Glucocorticids, Stress & Autoimmunity." *Journal of Steroid Bio Chemistry and Molecular Biology* 40: pp. 619–37.

hooks, bell. 1993. *Sisters of the Yam: Black Women and Self-Recovery.* Boston: South End Press.

———. 2001. *Salvation: Black People and Love.* New York: HarperCollins Perennial.

Horowitz, Janice. 2002. "10 Foods That Pack a Wallop." *New York Times Magazine,* 21 January, pp. 74–78.

Horton, A. J., ed. 1995. *The Women's Health Data Book: A Profile of Women's Health in the United States,* 2d ed. Washington, D.C.: The Jacobs Institute of Women's Health.

Hoskins, Nichele. 2000. "A Sister's Circle of Yoga." *Heart & Soul,* August/September, p. 28.

House, S. James. 1981. *Work Stress and Social Support.* Reading Mass.: Addison-Wesley.

Hull, Gloria, Patricia Bell Scott, and Barbara Smith. 1982. *All the Women Are White, All the Blacks Are Men, But Some of Us Are Brave.* Westbury, Conn.: The Feminist Press.

Iverson, D. B., and G. Scheer. 1987. *Changing Social Forces Concurrent with the Development of the Child.* Thorofare, N.J.: Slack.

Jibrin, Janis. 2000. "The Super Foods: Surprising Ways to Stay Well." *Women's Day,* 1 September, p. 129.

Johansen, C., and J. Olsen. 1997. "Psychological Stress, Cancer Incidence and Mortality from Non-Malignant Diseases." *British Journal of Cancer* 75, no. 1: pp. 144–48.

Johnson, K. 1996. "Balancing the Scale on Body Weight." *Health Quest: The Publication of Black Wellness.* Black History Special Issue 12, p. 10.

Justice, L. A. 2000a. *Beat Stress.* Boca Raton, Fla.: American Media Mini Mags.

———. 2000b. *Healing Juices.* Boca Raton, Fla.: American Media Mini Mags.

Kashef, Ziba. 1997. "To Your Health." *Essence,* December, pp. 32–36.

Katcher, A., A. Homore, B. Brythtman, L. Luborsky, and I. Ship. 1973. "Prediction of the Incidence of Recurrent Herpes Labialis and Systemic Illness from Psychological Measurements." *Journal of Dental Research* 52: pp. 49–58.

Katz, Judy. 1978. *White Awareness: Handbook for Anti Racism Training*. Norman: University of Oklahoma Press.

Keith, Verna. 1997. "Life Stress and Psychological Well-Being among Married and Unmarried Blacks." In *Family Life in Black America*, ed. Robert Taylor, James Jackson, and Linda Chattlers, pp. 95–117. New York: Sage Publications.

Keller, C. J., J. Fleury, and D. Bergstrom. 1995. "Risk Factors for Coronary Heart Disease in African American Women." *Cardiovascular Nursing* 31, no. 2 (March/April): pp. 9–14.

King, Angela. 2001. "Coca-Cola Takes the High Road." *Black Enterprise*, 3, no. 7 (February): p. 29.

Kisch, E. S. 1985. "Stressful Events and the Onset of Diabetes Mellitus." *Israel Journal of Medical Science*, no. 21: pp. 356–58.

Kovach, Sue. 2002. *Herbs That Work Better Than Drugs*. Boca Raton, Fla.: American Media Mini Mags.

Krause, Neal, and Thanh Van Tran. 1989. "Stress and Religious Involvement among Older Blacks." *Journal of Gerontology: Social Science*, 44, no. 1: pp. 4–13.

Lach, J. 2001. American Demographics: Minority Women Hit a Concrete Ceiling. http://www.britannica.com. Accessed October 11, 2001.

Lammermeier, Paul. 1973. "The Urban Black Family of the Nineteenth Century: A Study of Black Family Structure in the Ohio Valley 1850–1880." *Journal of Marriage and Family* 35, no. 3: pp. 440–57.

Lazarus, Judith. 1999. "Wondrous Watsu: Water Therapy for Mind, Body and Spirit." *Healing Retreats*, July/August, pp. 67–72.

Learum, E., G. Storvold, J. Suvele, L. Volker, P. Thune, and J. N. Brewin. 1991. "Recurrent Herpes Labialis and Secondary Bacterial Infection: A Study among the Employees at the Ulleval Hospital." *Tedsskrift Far Den Norske Loegeforening*. 111: pp. 1136–1368.

Lee See, Letha A. 1989. "Tension between Black Women and White Women: A Study." *Affilia: Journal of Women and Social Work* 4, no. 2 (Summer): pp. 31–45.

Lehrman, Sally. 2000. "Six Herbal Remedies That Really Work." *Readers Digest*, December, pp. 33–35.

LeShane, L. 1959. "Psychological State as Factor in the Development of Malignant Diseases: A Critical Review." *Journal of the National Cancer Institute* 22: pp. 1–18.

"Let's Make a Slave." 1970. Black Arcade Liberation Library. http://www.afrocentricnews.com/html/lynch.htm

Long, Delores. 2001. *Nature's Healing Secrets*. Boca Raton, Fla.: American Media Mini Mags.

Long, Patricia. 1992. "Can Foods Heal?" *Glamour*, November, pp. 270–71.

Longo, D. J., and G. A. Clum. 1989. "Psychosocial Factors Affecting Genital Herpes Recurrence." *Journal of Psychosomatic Research* 33: pp. 161–66.

Lovallo, William. 1997. *Stress and Health: Biological and Psychological Interactions*. Thousand Oaks, Calif.: Sage Publications.

Makosky, Vivian. 1982. "Sources of Stress Events or Conditions." In *Lives in Stress: Women and Depression*, ed. Deborah Belle, pp. 38–54. Beverly Hills, Calif.: Sage Publications.

Malveaux, J. 1997. "The Myth of Educational Attainment: When a Black Woman's Master's Equals a White Woman's Bachelor's Degree." *Black Issues in Higher Education*, 11 December, p. 33.

Manfred, Erica. 1996. "Co-Workers from Hell and How to Cope." *Cosmopolitan*, February, pp. 146–48.

Manson, Joann, Michael Shlepak, and Nanette Kass Wenger. 2001. "Heart Diseases in Older Women." *Patient Care for the Nurse Practitioner*, May, pp. 28–44.

Mathe, G. 1996. "Depression, Stressful Events and Risk of Cancer." *Biomedicine and Pharmacology* 50: pp. 1–2.

Maynard, C., N. Every, P. Letwin, J. Martin, and D. Weaver. 1995. "Outcomes on African American Women with Suspected Acute Myocardial Infarction: The Myocardial Infarction Triage and Intervention Project." *Journal of the National Medical Association* 87 no. 5: pp. 339–44.

McAdoo Pipes, Harriette. *Black Families*, 2d ed. Thousand Oaks, Calif.: Sage Publishing.

McGee, Zena. 2000. "The Pains of Imprisonment of Long Term Incarceration Effects on Women in Prison." In *It's a Crime: Women and Justice*, 2d ed., ed. Roslyn Muraskin, pp. 205–16. Upper Saddle River, N.J.: Prentice Hall.

McIntosh, Peggy. 1992. "White Privilege and Male Privilege." In *Anthology, Race, Class and Gender*, ed. M. Anderson and Patricia Collins, pp. 70–83. Belmont, Calif.: Wadsworth Publishing Company.

McKenzie, Vashti. 2001. *Leadership Development for Women: Strength in the Struggle*. Cleveland: The Pilgrim Press.

Miles, Elizabeth. 1997. *Tune Your Brain: Using Music to Manage Your Mind, Body and Mood*. New York: Berkeley Books.

Miller, Lyle, Alma Smith, and Larry Rothstein. 1993. *The Stress Solutions: Manage the Stress in Your Life*. New York: Life Pocket Books.

Misra, Dawn. 2001. *The Women's Health Data Book: A Profile of Women's Health in the United States*, 3d ed. Washington, D.C.: The Jacobs Institute of Women's Health.

Mitchell, Angela, and Kennise Herring. 1997. *What the Blues Is All About*. New York: Berkeley Publishing Group.

Morris-Prather, C. F., J. P. Harrel, R. Collins, M. Boss, and J. W. Lee. 1996. "Gender Differences in Mood and Cardiovascular Responses to Socially Stressful Stimuli." *Ethnicity and Diseases* 6, no. 1–2: pp. 123–33.

Moynihan, Daniel Patrick. 1965. "The Negro Family: The Case for National Action." Washington, D.C.: U.S. Government Printing Office.

Myers, Lena. 1991. *Black Women: Do They Cope Better?* San Francisco: Mellen Research University Press.

"Nature's Best Medicine: Foods That Fight Disease." 2002. *Family Circle*, 2 March, pp. 71–74.

"99 Herbal Cures for Women." 2001. *Women's Health Special, Prevention's Guide*, 26 January, pp. 16–77.

"Obesity." 2001. *Parents Magazine*, October, p. 67.

O'Brien, James. 1998. *Herbal Cures for Common Ailments*. New York: Globe Digest.

Powell, J. Robin, and Holly Warren-George. 1994. *The Working Woman's Guide to Managing Stress*. Englewood Cliffs, N.J.: Prentice Hall.

Prevention's Healing with Motion. 1999. Emmaus, Pa.: Rodale Press.

"Progress Slow for Minorities, Women among Ranks of College Presidents." 1998. *Black Issues in Higher Education,* 30 April, p. 8.

Quarles, Benjamin. 1969. *The Negro in the Making of America.* New York: Macmillan.

Rabkin, Rachel. 2002. "Herbal Remedies That Really Work." *Family Circle,* 11 November, centerfold.

Rawls, George, and Frank Lloyd. 2001. *Managing Cancer: The African American's Guide to Prevention, Diagnosis and Treatment.* Roscoe, Ill.: Hilton Publishing Company.

Raybon, Patricia. 1996. *My First White Friend.* New York: Penguin Books.

Reed, W., W. Darity, and N. Roberson. 1993. *Health and Medical Care of African Americans.* Westport, Conn.: Auburn House.

Roberts, F. D., P. A. Newcomb, A. Trenthan-Dietz, and B. E. Storer. 1996. "Self Reported Stress and Risk Factors of Breast Cancer." *Cancer* 77, no. 6: pp. 1089–93.

Rohlfing, Carla. 1991. "Anticancer Diet—What to Eat Now." *Family Circle,* 20 May, pp. 94–99.

Rosch, P. J. 1993. "Is Cancer Another Disease of Adoption? Some Insight into the Role and Civilization." *Comprehensive Therapy* 19, no. 5: pp. 183–87.

Sapolsky, Robert. 1990. *Why Zebras Don't Get Ulcers: A Guide to Stress Related Illnesses and Coping.* New York: Freeman Company.

Schmidt, D. D., S. Zyanski, J. Ellnet, M. L. Kiemar, and J. Aino. 1985. "Stress as a Precipitating Factor in Recurrent Herpes Labialis." *Journal of Family Practice* 20: pp. 359–66.

Scott, J. 1993. "Why Are Mortality Rates on the Rise for Black Women? *Vital Signs* Special Report Walking for Wellness, January/March.

Scott, Jones D., and Sharon Nelson-La Gall. 1986. "Defining Black Families: Past and Present." In *Redefining Social Problems,* eds. Edward Seedman and Julian Rapport, pp. 83–100. New York: Plenum Publishing.

Scott, Joseph, and Albert Black. 1991. "Deep Structure of African American Family Life: Female and Male Kin Network." In *The Black Family Essays and Studies,* ed. R. Staples, pp. 201–11. Belmont, Calif.: Wadsworth Publishers.

Scott, Kesho Yvonne. 1991. *The Habit of Surviving.* New Brunswick, N.J.: Rutgers University Press.

Scott, Matthew. 2001. "For Women the Glass Ceiling Persists." *Black Enterprise,* August, p. 30.

Selye, H. 1979. "Correlating Stress and Cancer." *Journal of Proctology, Gastroenterology, Colon and Rectal Surgery* 13 (July/August): pp. 18–28.

Shapiro, Joseph. 1995. "Does Affirmative Action Mean No White Men Need Apply." *U.S. News & World Report* 118, no. 16 (February 13): pp. 32–39.

Siegel, B. 1986. *Love, Medicine and Miracles.* New York: Harper and Row.

Slaby, Andrew. 1988. *Sixty Ways to Make Stress Work for You.* New York: The PIA Press.

Slawson, P. F., W. R. Flynn, and E. J. Kollar. 1963. "Psychological Factors Associated with Onset of Diabetes Mellitus." *Journal of the American Medical Association* no. 185: pp. 166–70.

Smoke, Sandra. 1997. "The Hill/Thomas Drama Raised Blacks' Stature." *USA Today,* 10 October, p. F2.

Snapp, Mary Beth. 1992. "Occupational Stress, Social Support, and Depression among Black and White Women Professional-Managerial Women." *Women and Health* 18, no. 1: pp. 41–79.

Spiegel, B. 1988. "Mind over Cancer." *Prevention,* March, pp. 59–64.

Spiegel, B., J. R. Bloom, and H. Kraemer. 1993. "The Effect of Psychosocial Behavior," *Lancet* 2, pp. 888–991.

Stanley, Louise. 2002. *Garlic, Vinegar and Honey.* Boca Raton, Fla.: American Media Mini Mags.

Staples, Robert. 1991. *The Black Family: Essays and Studies.* Belmont, Calif.: Wadsworth Publishers.

Starling, Kelly. 1999. "Black Women and the Blues." *Ebony,* May, pp. 140–44.

Statistical Abstract of the United States. 1998. Washington D.C.: U.S. Department of Commerce, Bureau of the Census, Bureau of Labor Statistics. January, Table 61.

Sterling, Dorothy. 1984. *We Are Sisters: Black Women in the Nineteenth Century.* New York. W. W. Norton and Company.

Stevenson, C. 1999. "The Miseducation of Danielle Johnson." *The Challenger News,* 24 March, p. 3.

Stout, C., and W. Bloom. 1986. "Genital Herpes and Personality." *Journal of Human Stress* 12: pp. 119–124.

"Stress and Strain on Black Women." 1974. *Ebony,* June, pp. 33–36.

Taylor, Ronald, ed. 1994. *Minority Families in the United States: A Multicultural Perspective,* pp. 19–37. Englewood Cliffs, N.J.: Prentice Hall.

Taylor, R., S. Jackson, and L. Chatters. 1997. *Family Life in Black America.* New York: Sage Publications.

Taylor, Susan. 1993. *In The Spirit.* New York: Essence Communication Inc.

"To All Who Believe in Me." 2001. Church Bulletin, Israel African Methodist Episcopal Church, Rev. Harold Rutherford. Albany, New York, 18 February.

Tharp, Mike. 1995. "Affirmative Action on the Edge," *US News & World Report* 118, no. 6: pp. 32–47.

Tierney, T. 1988. "Wired for Stress." *New York Times Magazine,* 15 May, pp. 47–49.

Toliver, Susan. 1998. *Black Families in Corporate America.* Thousand Oaks, Calif.: Sage Publications.

"Top 10 in 1991." 1991. *US News & World Report,* 20 May, pp. 94–99.

Walcott-McQuigg, J. A. 1995. "The Relationship between Stress and Weight Control in African American Women." *Journal of the National Medical Association* 87, no. 6 (June): pp. 427–32.

Ward, B. 1997. *Health Tips.* Boca Raton, Fla.: Globe Communication Group.

———. 2000. *Think Yourself Well.* Boca Raton, Fla.: Globe Digest.

Weathers, Diane Marie. 1997. "Corporate Race War." *Essence,* October, p. 80–84.

———. 1998. "Death of a Superwomen." *Essence,* March, pp. 82–84.

Webb, M. S., K. A. Smyth, and H. Yarandi. 2000. "A Progressive Relaxation Intervention at the Workplace for African American Women," *Journal of the National Black Nurses Association* 2, pp. 1–6.

Wegman, E. M. 1990. "Annual Summary of Vital Statistics 1989." *Pediatrics* 8, no. 6: Table 4, p. 841.

———. 1993. "Annual Summary of Vital Statistics 1992." *Pediatrics* 92, no. 6: Table 4, p. 747.

Weiner, F. Morli. 1995. *Mistress and Slaves: Plantation Women in South Carolina.* Champaign: University of Illinois Press.

Whitcare, C. W., S. Cummings, and A. C. Griffin. 1994. The Effects of Stress on Autoimmune Diseases. In *Handbook of Human Stress and Immunity,* ed. C. Glaser and J. Krecolt, pp. 78–84. Columbus, Ohio: Academic Press.

Wildwood, C. 1997. *The Complete Guide to Reducing Stress.* London: Judy Piatkus Publishers.

Williams, E. 1999. "The Use of Herbs As Remedial Alternatives Treatment to Conventional Medicine." Master's thesis, State University of New York, Empire State College.

Williams, N. A., and J. L. Deffenbacker. 1983. "Life Stress and Chronic Yeast Infection." *Journal of Human Stress* 9: pp. 26–31.

Wilson, M., and K. Russell. 1996. *Divided Sisters.* New York: Doubleday/Anchor Books.

Woods, Theodore. 1998. "Is Affirmative Action Still Needed?" *University of Dayton Law Journal*: Race and Racism. www.odayton.edu/race/annotated /98woods.html. Accessed November 2001.

Worthington, Cassandra. 1992. "An Examination of Factors Influencing the Diagnosis and Treatment of Black Patients in Mental Health Systems." *Archives of Psychiatric Nursing* 6: pp. 195–204.

Index

.

About the Author

CATHERINE FISHER COLLINS is an associate professor of Community and Human Services at the State University of New York, Empire State College. She is also adjunct professor in the Women's Studies Department at the State University of New York and immediate past National Vice President for Jack and Jill of America, Inc., an organization for African American families.